VIENNA TRAVEL GUIDE 2023 AND BEYOND

Embrace the Imperial Splendor of Austria's Capital

By: Sophie Fischer

Copyright © 2023 Sophie Fischer

All rights reserved.

Without the proper written consent of the publisher and copyright owner, this book cannot be used or distributed in any way, shape, or form, except for brief quotations used in a review. This book should not be considered a substitute for medical, legal, or other professional advice.

Contents

INTRODUCTION	1
TRAVEL PRACTICALITIES	3
Basic Information	3
Accommodation options	6
25 Travel Tips	9
HISTORY OF VIENNA	13
Ancient and Roman Times	13
Medieval Era	13
Renaissance and Baroque Period	14
Ottoman Sieges	14
Age of Enlightenment	14
Congress of Vienna and Austro-Hungarian Empire	14
World Wars and Interwar Period	15
Cold War and Austrian Neutrality	15
Modern Vienna	15
HISTORICAL SITES	16
Rathaus (Vienna City Hall)	16
Austrian National Library	19
Maria am Gestade	22
Capuchin Crypt	24

Albertina	26
Judenplatz Holocaust Memorial	29
Vienna's Ringstrasse	31
Vienna's Jewish Heritage	35
BEST TOURS AND ACTIVITIES	38
An Evening of Elegance	38
Day Trip from Vienna to the Wachau Valley	40
Pedal Through History on a Bike and City Tour	42
Embark on a Journey from Vienna to Hallstatt	44
A Celebration of Pastries and Delights	45
Hop-On Hop-Off Freedom	48
A 3-Hour Journey through Schönbrunn Palace	50
The Spanish Riding School Experience	51
IMPERIAL PALACES AND SITES	54
Schönbrunn Palace (Schloss Schönbrunn)	54
Hofburg Palace	57
Belvedere Palace (Schloss Belvedere)	60
Schloss Hetzendorf	63
Imperial Crypt (Kapuzinergruft)	65
The Vienna Residence Orchestra	67
Apothecary Museum of the Vienna General Hospital	70
Kaisergruft (Imperial Burial Vault)	73
MUSEUM AND GALLERIES	76

Belvedere Palace and Museum	76
Albertina Museum and Art Gallery	79
Leopold Museum	81
Kunsthistorisches Museum (Museum of Art History)	84
MAK - Austrian Museum of Applied Arts/Contemporary Art	87
MuseumQuartier (MQ)	89
Secession Building	92
Vienna State Opera Museum	94
Ludwig Foundation Vienna	96
ARCHITECTURAL MARVELS	99
St. Stephen's Cathedral (Stephansdom)	99
Vienna State Opera (Wiener Staatsoper)	102
Hundertwasserhaus	105
Austrian Parliament Building (Parlament)	108
Karlskirche (St. Charles's Church)	110
Secession Building: Art Nouveau Showcase	113
ROYAL GARDENS AND PARKS	116
Schönbrunn Palace Gardens	117
Belvedere Gardens	120
Hofburg Palace Gardens	122
Augarten	126
Lainzer Tiergarten	129

Stadtpark	131
Schoenbrunn Palace Park	134
Prater Park	137
Volksgarten	140
MUSIC AND CULTURE	143
Music Heritage	143
Theater And Performances	146
Vienna State Opera	149
Haus der Musik (House of Music)	152
Wolfgang Amadeus Mozart	155
Ludwig van Beethoven	156
Cultural Events	157
COFFEE CULTURE AND CUISINE	161
Traditional Coffeehouses	162
Naschmarkt	164
Coffee Specialties	167
Viennese Sachertorte	169
ACTIVITIES	172
Strolls and Hikes	172
Cruises	175
Biking	177
Horse-Drawn Carriage Rides	180
Romantic Activities	182

Visit Vienna's Wine Taverns	185
Outdoor Activities	188
Water Sports	191
Kid-Friendly Activities	193
Group Activities	196
DAY TRIPS AND EXCURSIONS	200
Wachau Valley	200
Schönbrunn Palace and Gardens	201
Bratislava, Slovakia	201
Salzburg	202
Budapest, Hungary	202
Lake Neusiedl	202
Graz	203
Eisenstadt	203
Carnuntum Archaeological Park	203
Lower Austria's Wine Regions	203
ITINERARIES	204
Wachau Valley Delights	204
Imperial and Artistic Treasures	204
Musical Salzburg Experience	205
Budapest Breeze	205
Nature and Culture in Lower Austria	206
Graz Adventure	206

Historical Carnuntum and Roman Remains	206
Wine Regions Discovery	207
Thermenregion Wellness and Culture	207
Danube Magic in Krems and Klosterneuburg	208
MAPS	209
Vienna City Map	209
Wachau Valley Map	210
Accommodations Map	211
Restaurants Map	212
Shopping Map	213
CONCLUSION	214
INDEX	215

INTRODUCTION

Willkommen in Wien! Welcome to Vienna, the resplendent capital of Austria where imperial grandeur, artistic treasures, and cultural opulence converge. As we step into Vienna in 2023 and beyond, we invite you to immerse yourself in a city that resonates with the echoes of classical music, showcases architectural marvels, and preserves a legacy of royalty and refinement.

Vienna, often referred to as the "City of Music" and the "City of Dreams," beckons you to stroll along its elegant boulevards, admire its baroque palaces, and revel in the harmonious blend of history and modernity. From the majestic Schönbrunn Palace to the ornate interiors of St. Stephen's Cathedral, the city reflects the splendor of its Habsburg heritage. Whether you're sipping coffee in a traditional café or attending a performance at the Vienna State Opera, Vienna promises an enchanting experience that will awaken your senses and ignite your cultural curiosity.

In this travel guide, we will delve into the heart of Vienna's imperial splendor and beyond, uncovering its hidden treasures, celebrating its artistic legacy, and inviting you to embrace a city that has shaped the world of music, art, and intellect.

TRAVEL PRACTICALITIES

Traveling to a new destination like Vienna requires some practical considerations to ensure a smooth and enjoyable trip. Here are some travel practicalities to keep in mind when planning your visit to Vienna:

Basic Information

Visa and Entry Requirements:

Check whether you need a visa to enter Austria and ensure that your passport is valid for at least six months beyond your planned return date. Citizens of the EU and many other countries do not need a visa for short stays.

Currency:

The official currency in Austria is the Euro (EUR). Make sure to have some local currency on hand for small purchases, and consider informing your bank about your travel plans to avoid any issues with using your credit/debit cards abroad.

Language:

The official language in Vienna is German. While many locals speak English, it's helpful to learn a few basic phrases in German or have a translation app handy.

Transportation:

- ❖ **Public Transportation:** Vienna has an efficient public transportation system, including trams, buses, and the U-Bahn (subway). Purchase a Vienna Card for unlimited rides on public transport and discounts at attractions.

- ❖ **Vienna City Bikes:** The city offers a bike-sharing system, making it easy to explore on two wheels.

- ❖ **Taxis and Ride-Sharing:** Taxis are readily available, but ride-sharing services like Uber are also popular.

Safety and Health:

Vienna is generally safe for travelers, but it's wise to take standard safety precautions. Ensure you have travel insurance that covers medical expenses and emergency situations.

Weather:

Vienna experiences four distinct seasons. Check the weather forecast for your travel dates and pack accordingly. Layers are recommended, as the weather can be unpredictable.

Electrical Outlets:

Austria uses Type C and Type F electrical outlets, with a standard voltage of 230V and a frequency of 50Hz. Consider bringing a universal travel adapter if your devices have different plug types.

Tipping:

Tipping is customary in restaurants, and it's typical to round up the bill or leave a 5-10% tip.

Dress Code:

Vienna is relatively formal. When visiting churches or upscale restaurants, consider dressing more conservatively.

Time Zone:

Vienna is in the Central European Time Zone (CET), which is UTC+1. The city observes Daylight Saving Time, moving to Central European Summer Time (CEST) during the warmer months (UTC+2).

Wi-Fi and Connectivity:

Wi-Fi is commonly available in hotels, cafes, and public places. If you need mobile data, consider getting a local SIM card or an international data plan from your provider.

Accommodation options

Vienna offers a diverse range of accommodation options to cater to different preferences and budgets. Whether you're looking for luxury hotels, boutique stays, budget-friendly hostels, or cozy guesthouses, you'll find a variety of choices to suit your needs. Here are some types of accommodation options in Vienna:

Luxury Hotels:

Vienna is home to several luxurious hotels that provide top-notch amenities, excellent service, and a touch of elegance. Many of these hotels are located in historic buildings and offer fine dining, spa facilities, and concierge services.

Boutique Hotels:

For a more personalized experience, consider staying in a boutique hotel. These smaller establishments often boast unique designs, themed rooms, and a cozy atmosphere that sets them apart from chain hotels.

Historic Palaces and Grand Hotels:

Experience the city's imperial past by staying in a historic palace or grand hotel. These properties offer opulent interiors, lavish suites, and a taste of Viennese aristocracy.

Apartment Rentals:

Renting an apartment can provide a more homey and independent experience. Many apartments come equipped with kitchens and living spaces, making them ideal for families or travelers who prefer to cook their meals.

Guesthouses and Pensionen:

Guesthouses and pensionen (boarding houses) offer a more intimate and local atmosphere. They often provide a homely ambiance, personalized service, and the opportunity to interact with the hosts.

Hostels:

Vienna has a selection of well-maintained hostels that cater to budget travelers and backpackers. These accommodations offer shared dormitory-style rooms, communal spaces, and a chance to meet fellow travelers.

Bed and Breakfasts:

Bed and breakfast accommodations offer a comfortable stay with a hearty morning meal included. They are often located in residential neighborhoods, providing a glimpse into local life.

Design and Art Hotels:

Art enthusiasts might enjoy staying in a design or art-themed hotel. These properties often showcase contemporary art, innovative architecture, and creative interior designs.

Wellness and Spa Hotels:

If relaxation is a priority, consider booking a wellness or spa hotel. These accommodations offer rejuvenating spa treatments, wellness facilities, and a focus on overall well-being.

Green and Sustainable Accommodations:

For environmentally conscious travelers, there are accommodations that prioritize sustainability and eco-friendly practices, such as minimizing waste and conserving energy.

25 Travel Tips

Here are 25 travel tips to help you make the most of your trip to Vienna and ensure a smooth and enjoyable experience:

Before You Go:

1. **Research:** Familiarize yourself with Vienna's attractions, culture, and local customs before your trip.

2. **Travel Insurance:** Obtain comprehensive travel insurance that covers medical emergencies, trip cancellations, and lost belongings.

3. **Visa Requirements:** Check if you need a visa to enter Austria and ensure your passport has sufficient validity.

4. **Health Precautions:** Consult your doctor for recommended vaccinations and medications based on your health and travel plans.

5. **Currency:** Exchange some currency or inform your bank about your travel dates to ensure smooth credit/debit card usage.

Packing:

6. **Weather-Appropriate Clothing:** Pack clothing suitable for the weather during your travel dates, and consider layers for temperature changes.

7. **Comfortable Shoes:** Vienna is a city for walking, so bring comfortable walking shoes.

8. **Electrical Adapters:** Carry the necessary adapters to charge your devices using Austrian electrical outlets.

9. **Travel Essentials:** Pack essentials like a travel adapter, medications, toiletries, a small first aid kit, and a universal charger.

10. **Important Documents:** Keep copies of your passport, visa, travel insurance, and emergency contact numbers in a separate place.

Getting Around:

11. **Public Transport:** Use Vienna's efficient public transportation system, including trams, buses, and the U-Bahn (subway).

12. **Vienna Card:** Consider purchasing a Vienna Card for unlimited public transport rides and discounts at attractions.

13. **City Bikes:** Explore the city on two wheels with Vienna's bike-sharing system.

14. **Navigation Apps:** Download offline maps and navigation apps to easily find your way around.

Sightseeing:

15. **Skip-the-Line Tickets:** Purchase skip-the-line tickets for popular attractions to save time and avoid long queues.

16. **City Passes:** Look into city passes that offer discounted access to multiple attractions.

17. **Guided Tours:** Join guided tours to gain insights and a deeper understanding of Vienna's history and culture.

Cultural Etiquette:

18. **Greetings:** Greet locals with a polite "Guten Tag" (Good day) or "Grüß Gott" (common in Austria).

19. **Tipping:** It's customary to leave a 5-10% tip at restaurants. Round up for small purchases.

Dining and Drinking:

20. **Viennese Cuisine:** Try traditional dishes like Wiener Schnitzel and Sachertorte.

21. **Café Culture:** Immerse yourself in Vienna's coffeehouse culture and enjoy coffee and pastries.

22. **Tap Water:** Vienna has high-quality tap water, so consider carrying a reusable water bottle.

Safety and Health:

23. **Emergency Numbers:** Save local emergency numbers and your embassy's contact information.

24. **Safety Precautions:** Stay cautious of your belongings, especially in crowded areas.

25. **COVID-19 Precautions:** Check local guidelines, restrictions, and requirements related to the pandemic before and during your trip.

HISTORY OF VIENNA

Vienna's history is rich and complex, spanning centuries of cultural, political, and artistic developments. Here's an overview of Vienna's history from its early origins to the present day:

Ancient and Roman Times

Vienna's history dates back to ancient times when the area was inhabited by Celtic and Roman settlements. The Romans established a military camp called "Vindobona" in the 1st century AD near what is now the historic city center.

Medieval Era

Vienna's importance grew during the Middle Ages as it became a center for trade and commerce. In 1278, the Habsburg dynasty began its long association with the city when Rudolf I chose Vienna as his residence. Vienna's city walls were built, and the city became an important political and cultural hub.

Renaissance and Baroque Period

Vienna flourished during the Renaissance and Baroque eras. The Habsburg rulers, especially Emperor Charles VI and his daughter Maria Theresa, transformed the city into a magnificent imperial capital. Impressive palaces, such as Schönbrunn and Belvedere, were built during this time.

Ottoman Sieges

In the 16th and 17th centuries, Vienna faced two Ottoman sieges (1529 and 1683) that marked significant events in the city's history. The sieges were repelled with the help of alliances and contributed to the city's role in protecting Central Europe from Ottoman expansion.

Age of Enlightenment

During the 18th century, Vienna became a cultural center of the Age of Enlightenment. Composers like Wolfgang Amadeus Mozart and Ludwig van Beethoven lived and worked in the city, contributing to its reputation as a city of music and arts.

Congress of Vienna and Austro-Hungarian Empire

Vienna played a crucial role in shaping European politics during the Congress of Vienna in 1814-1815, which aimed to redraw the map of Europe after the Napoleonic Wars. The city then became the capital of the Austro-Hungarian Empire, an expansive multinational monarchy.

World Wars and Interwar Period

Vienna faced challenges during both World War I and World War II. After the collapse of the Austro-Hungarian Empire, Vienna became the capital of a smaller Austria. During World War II, it was annexed by Nazi Germany and subsequently liberated by Allied forces.

Cold War and Austrian Neutrality

After World War II, Vienna was divided into zones controlled by the four Allied powers. The city later became a symbol of East-West tensions during the Cold War. Austria declared neutrality in 1955, ensuring it remained independent and unaligned.

Modern Vienna

In recent decades, Vienna has continued to thrive as a cultural capital. The city's historic architecture, music scene, and vibrant arts culture attract visitors from around the world. Vienna has also hosted various international organizations and events, including the United Nations Office at Vienna.

HISTORICAL SITES

Vienna is a city steeped in history, and it boasts a wealth of historical sites that offer a glimpse into its rich past. From imperial palaces to ancient churches, each site has its own unique story to tell. Here are some of Vienna's most notable historical sites:

Rathaus (Vienna City Hall)

Vienna's Rathaus, or City Hall, is a striking architectural masterpiece that stands as a testament to the city's history and civic identity. This magnificent Neo-Gothic building is not only a center of local government but also a symbol of Vienna's grandeur and cultural heritage. Here's a closer look at the enchanting Vienna City Hall:

Neo-Gothic Splendor:

The Rathaus is a prime example of Neo-Gothic architecture, characterized by its intricate stone carvings, pointed arches, and ornate details. The building's design draws inspiration from historical Gothic architecture while incorporating modern elements.

Historical Background:

Construction of the Rathaus began in the late 19th century and was completed in the early 20th century. The building was intended to reflect Vienna's status as a growing and influential capital city during the Austro-Hungarian Empire.

Main Facade and Towers:

The Rathaus features a central tower that rises above the building and is adorned with statues and decorative elements. The facade is adorned with allegorical figures, statues of historical figures, and ornate reliefs that represent various aspects of Viennese life and history.

City Council Chamber:

The Rathaus houses the City Council Chamber, where important civic decisions are made. The chamber's design is in keeping with the building's Neo-Gothic style.

Festive Illumination:

The Rathaus is known for its beautiful illumination during special occasions, particularly during the Christmas season when it serves as the backdrop for the Vienna Christmas Market.

Events and Functions:

The Rathaus hosts a range of events, exhibitions, and cultural activities throughout the year, contributing to its role as a vibrant civic and cultural hub.

Rathausplatz:

The square in front of the Rathaus, known as Rathausplatz, is often used for public gatherings, events, and festivals. During the summer, it hosts open-air film screenings, concerts, and other entertainment.

Austrian National Library

The Austrian National Library, located in the heart of Vienna within the Hofburg Palace complex, is not only a repository of knowledge but also a masterpiece of Baroque architecture. This library is a treasure trove of books, manuscripts, and historical artifacts that offer insights into Austria's cultural heritage and intellectual pursuits. Here's a closer look at the enchanting Austrian National Library:

Historical Significance:

The library was founded in the late 16th century and has since evolved into one of the world's most important research and cultural institutions.

It was originally established as the Imperial Court Library to serve the Habsburg dynasty and the imperial court.

Baroque Architecture:

The library's State Hall, known as the "Prunksaal," is a stunning example of Baroque design. The hall features elaborately decorated ceilings, frescoes, gilded stucco work, and magnificent bookcases. The grandeur of the architecture creates an atmosphere that immerses visitors in the splendor of the past.

Collections and Exhibitions:

The Austrian National Library houses a vast collection of books, manuscripts, maps, and artwork spanning centuries.

Notable items in the collection include the "Prayer Book of Emperor Maximilian I" and the "Gutenberg Bible," one of the earliest printed books. Temporary exhibitions are often held within the library, showcasing rare and valuable items from its extensive holdings.

State Hall Tours:

Visitors can explore the State Hall on guided tours, which provide insights into the library's history, architecture, and notable works. The tours allow visitors to marvel at the beauty of the hall while learning about the cultural significance of the library.

Globes and Curiosities:

The library's Globenmuseum (Globe Museum) houses a remarkable collection of globes, celestial maps, and navigational instruments from different eras. It offers a unique perspective on the evolution of cartography and our understanding of the world.

Cultural Hub:

The Austrian National Library is not only a place of research and preservation but also a cultural hub that hosts events, lectures, and discussions related to literature, history, and art.

Visiting Tips:

Check the library's website for information on opening hours, guided tours, and special exhibitions. Photography restrictions may apply within certain areas of the library. The library's location within the Hofburg Palace complex makes it convenient to combine your visit with exploring other historical sites nearby.

Maria am Gestade

Maria am Gestade, a medieval church nestled in the heart of Vienna, is a hidden gem that offers a glimpse into the city's rich history and architectural heritage. This Gothic masterpiece has stood the test of time, surviving centuries of change while preserving its unique charm and spiritual significance. Here's a closer look at the enchanting Maria am Gestade:

Historical Significance:

Maria am Gestade, translated as "Mary on the Banks," dates back to the 14th century and is one of Vienna's oldest and most well-preserved churches. Its location near the Danube River has contributed to its name, which reflects its proximity to the water's edge.

Gothic Architecture:

The church's architecture is a prime example of Austrian Gothic style, characterized by its pointed arches, ribbed vaults, and ornate tracery.

The exterior features intricate stone carvings and statues that depict biblical scenes, saints, and religious symbols.

Interior Splendor:

The interior of Maria am Gestade is equally impressive, with a soaring nave, elegant columns, and a sense of spiritual solemnity. The church's stained glass windows filter light into the space, creating an ethereal atmosphere that invites contemplation.

High Altar and Altarpieces:

The high altar, dedicated to the Virgin Mary, is adorned with a detailed altarpiece that portrays the Coronation of Mary by angels and saints.

Other altarpieces within the church depict scenes from the life of Christ and the lives of various saints.

Historical Artifacts:

Maria am Gestade houses a collection of historical artifacts, including religious sculptures, paintings, and decorative elements that reflect the church's long history.

Spiritual Haven:

The church's serene ambiance and historical resonance make it a place of quiet reflection and spiritual solace for both locals and visitors.

Visiting Tips:

Maria am Gestade is open to the public, allowing visitors to admire its architectural and artistic treasures. While visiting, be sure to take in the details of the stone carvings, sculptures, and stained glass windows that adorn the church.

Capuchin Crypt

The Capuchin Crypt, located beneath the Capuchin Church in Vienna, is a unique and somber site that offers a glimpse into the final resting places of Habsburg royalty. This crypt has been the burial site for members of the Austrian imperial family for centuries, providing a space where history, art, and mortality converge. Here's a closer look at the solemn beauty of the Capuchin Crypt:

Historical Significance:

The Capuchin Crypt has been the chosen burial place for many Habsburg emperors, empresses, and other members of the imperial family since the 17th century. The crypt has witnessed the burials of notable figures, including Emperor Franz Joseph and Empress Elisabeth (Sisi).

Layout and Atmosphere:

The crypt consists of a series of vaulted chambers, each containing the sarcophagi and coffins of various Habsburg rulers and their family members. The somber ambiance of the crypt invites visitors to reflect on the passage of time and the mortality of even the most powerful individuals.

Imperial Tombs:

The crypt features ornate tombs adorned with elaborate sculptures and intricate details, reflecting the status and importance of the individuals interred within. The tombs provide insights into the styles and aesthetics of different historical periods.

Emperor Franz Joseph and Empress Elisabeth:

Perhaps the most visited tombs in the crypt are those of Emperor Franz Joseph and Empress Elisabeth, who had a profound impact on Austrian history and culture. Their tombs are adorned with symbolic representations and artistic elements that pay tribute to their lives.

Monuments and Symbols:

The crypt also houses various monuments and plaques dedicated to different members of the imperial family, each telling a story of their legacy and contributions.

Guided Tours:

Guided tours are available to provide insights into the history of the crypt, the Habsburg dynasty, and the individuals buried there. The tours offer context and historical narratives that enhance the experience of visiting this unique site.

Visiting Tips:

The crypt is open to the public, but it's recommended to check the opening hours and tour availability in advance. Photography may be restricted within certain areas of the crypt, so it's advisable to respect the rules.

Albertina

The Albertina, located in the heart of Vienna, is a world-renowned museum and cultural institution that houses an extensive collection of art, drawings, prints, and photographs. This historic palace-turned-museum offers visitors the opportunity to explore a diverse range of artistic works spanning centuries and styles. Here's a closer look at the captivating Albertina:

Historical Background:

The Albertina is named after Maria Christina, Duchess of Teschen, who resided in the palace in the 18th century and amassed a significant art collection. The museum was opened to the public in the 19th century, showcasing the art collection of the Habsburg family.

Collection Highlights:

The Albertina boasts an impressive array of artworks, including masterpieces by renowned artists such as Leonardo da Vinci, Michelangelo, Raphael, Rembrandt, and Albrecht Dürer. The museum's collection covers a wide range of genres, from Old Master paintings to modern and contemporary art.

Graphic Arts and Drawings:

The museum is particularly famous for its extensive collection of drawings, prints, and graphic art, with over a million works spanning from the Renaissance to the present day. The Graphic Arts collection offers a glimpse into the creative process and includes sketches, studies, and finished works by famous artists.

Temporary Exhibitions:

The Albertina hosts temporary exhibitions that showcase various themes, styles, and artists, ensuring that there's always something new to discover.

State Rooms and Architecture:

The museum's State Rooms provide visitors with insights into the grandeur of the former palace, offering a glimpse into the lifestyle of the Habsburg elite. The architecture of the building itself is a blend of Baroque and Neoclassical styles, providing an elegant backdrop for the art it houses.

Photographic Collection:

In addition to its art collections, the Albertina also houses an extensive photographic collection that spans the history of photography, from its inception to the present day.

Visiting Tips:

Check the museum's website for information on opening hours, current exhibitions, and admission prices. Audio guides and guided tours are available to enhance your experience and provide insights into the artworks on display.

Judenplatz Holocaust Memorial

The Judenplatz Holocaust Memorial, located in the heart of Vienna, serves as a solemn tribute to the memory of the Jewish victims of the Holocaust. This powerful and thought-provoking memorial is a reminder of the atrocities of the past and a call for remembrance, understanding, and tolerance. Here's a closer look at the significance of the Judenplatz Holocaust Memorial:

Historical Context:

The memorial is situated in Judenplatz, an area that holds historical significance as the center of Vienna's medieval Jewish Quarter. The memorial serves as a stark reminder of the tragic fate of Vienna's Jewish population during the Holocaust.

Design and Symbolism:

Designed by British artist Rachel Whiteread, the memorial consists of a concrete cube that stands as an empty library, symbolizing the absence of knowledge and culture resulting from the Holocaust. The external surface of the cube features imprints of books, representing the books that were burned during the Nazi regime's book burnings.

The "Nameless Library":

The memorial is often referred to as the "Nameless Library" due to the absence of titles or authors on the book spines. This lack of identity speaks to the countless lives lost and the eradication of individual histories.

Subterranean Space:

Visitors can descend into an underground chamber beneath the cube, where they encounter an exhibition that provides historical context, personal stories, and information about the Jewish community's fate during the Holocaust.

Remembrance and Reflection:

The Judenplatz Holocaust Memorial invites visitors to engage in reflection and remembrance, encouraging dialogue about the past and the importance of preventing such horrors from recurring.

A Message of Tolerance:

The memorial also serves as a message of tolerance, underscoring the importance of embracing diversity, promoting understanding, and standing against prejudice and hatred.

Visiting Tips:

The memorial is open to the public and accessible year-round. Admission is free. Plan to spend time both outside, contemplating the memorial's design and symbolism, and inside the subterranean exhibition to gain a comprehensive understanding of its significance.

Vienna's Ringstrasse

Vienna's Ringstrasse, often referred to simply as "the Ring," is a magnificent circular boulevard that encircles the historic city center. This grand avenue is lined with impressive buildings, parks, monuments, and cultural landmarks, showcasing Vienna's architectural and cultural richness. Here's a closer look at the significance and attractions of Vienna's Ringstrasse:

Historical Context:

The construction of the Ringstrasse began in the mid-19th century as part of an urban planning project that aimed to modernize Vienna and create a showcase of imperial architecture. The Ringstrasse replaced the city's old defensive walls and moats and transformed Vienna into a modern capital with a blend of architectural styles.

Architectural Diversity:

The Ringstrasse is home to a diverse range of architectural styles, including Neo-Renaissance, Neo-Baroque, Neo-Gothic, and Art Nouveau.

The buildings along the Ringstrasse were constructed to house government offices, cultural institutions, museums, and grand residences.

Vienna State Opera:

A renowned opera house that hosts world-class performances and stands as a symbol of Vienna's cultural heritage.

Hofburg Palace:

The former imperial palace complex that includes the Austrian President's residence, museums, and historical buildings.

Museum of Art History (Kunsthistorisches Museum):

An exquisite museum that houses an extensive collection of fine art and historical artifacts.

Natural History Museum (Naturhistorisches Museum):

A twin to the Museum of Art History, housing a remarkable collection of natural history specimens.

Parliament Building (Parlament):

An impressive Neo-Greek structure that serves as the seat of Austria's parliament.

Rathaus (Vienna City Hall):

A striking Neo-Gothic building that is both a seat of government and a cultural landmark.

Burgtheater:

A historic theater that has hosted countless theatrical performances, reflecting Vienna's rich cultural scene.

University of Vienna (Universität Wien):

One of the oldest universities in the German-speaking world, with a history dating back to 1365.

Votive Church (Votivkirche):

A stunning Neo-Gothic church that was built as a votive offering after an assassination attempt on Emperor Franz Joseph.

Parks and Green Spaces:

Alongside the buildings, the Ringstrasse features green spaces and parks where locals and visitors can relax, walk, and enjoy the city's beauty.

The Burggarten, Volksgarten, and Stadtpark are among the notable parks along the Ring.

Tram Tours and Promenades:

Visitors can explore the Ringstrasse on foot, by bicycle, or by taking one of the historical trams that run along the boulevard.

The Ringstrasse offers a picturesque setting for leisurely strolls and admiring the architectural landmarks.

Vienna's Jewish Heritage

Vienna's Jewish heritage is a profound and intricate part of the city's history, contributing to its cultural diversity, intellectual vibrancy, and artistic legacy. From the medieval Jewish Quarter to its contemporary Jewish community, Vienna's Jewish heritage is a rich tapestry that spans centuries. Here's a closer look at the significance and highlights of Vienna's Jewish heritage:

Medieval Roots:

Vienna's medieval Jewish Quarter, located around Judenplatz, was a center of Jewish life and commerce from the Middle Ages.

The area housed synagogues, religious institutions, and a thriving Jewish community until the tragic events of the Black Death in the 14th century.

Jewish Museum Vienna:

The Jewish Museum Vienna offers a comprehensive exploration of Jewish history, culture, and religion in Austria.

The museum's exhibits cover various periods, including the Middle Ages, the Habsburg era, and the Holocaust.

Judenplatz Holocaust Memorial:

Situated in Judenplatz, this poignant memorial commemorates the thousands of Austrian Jews who perished in the Holocaust. The memorial serves as a reminder of the tragedy and a call for remembrance and tolerance.

Synagogues and Religious Sites:

The Stadttempel, a functioning synagogue, survived the Holocaust and stands as a testament to Vienna's Jewish community.

Other synagogues, such as the Leopoldstadt Synagogue, have also played significant roles in the city's history.

Sigmund Freud:

The famous psychoanalyst Sigmund Freud was born and lived in Vienna. His former residence, now the Sigmund Freud Museum, offers insights into his life and work.

Contributions to Art and Culture:

Jewish artists, writers, and musicians have made significant contributions to Vienna's cultural landscape. The composer Gustav Mahler, for example, was of Jewish heritage and left an indelible mark on Vienna's music scene.

Contemporary Jewish Community:

Vienna's Jewish community is vibrant and diverse, encompassing various cultural, religious, and social aspects. Synagogues, community centers, and events contribute to a sense of continuity and connection.

Kadaververein:

The Kadaververein was an organization established by Jewish doctors in the early 20th century to provide affordable healthcare to Vienna's poor.

Vienna's Coffeehouse Culture:

Many of Vienna's historic coffeehouses, such as Café Central and Café Landtmann, were gathering places for Jewish intellectuals, artists, and writers.

Visiting Tips:

Explore the Jewish Museum Vienna and its exhibits to gain a comprehensive understanding of Vienna's Jewish history.

Take guided tours that focus on Jewish heritage to delve deeper into the historical sites and their significance.

BEST TOURS AND ACTIVITIES

In the heart of Vienna, a realm of cultural treasures and historical marvels awaits your discovery. Each tour is a chapter in this captivating narrative, offering a unique perspective on the city's grandeur, history, and charm. Embark on a journey that transcends time and space, as we introduce you to the top 8 tours that promise to immerse you in Vienna's soul and essence.

An Evening of Elegance

A Culinary Prelude:

In the heart of Vienna, an evening of opulence and refinement awaits. Begin your experience with a culinary journey at the esteemed Restaurant Bristol. Indulge in a sumptuous 3-course dinner, a symphony of Austrian flavors that pay homage to the country's rich gastronomic heritage. As you savor each exquisite bite, you'll be transported to a realm of culinary artistry.

Dine Amidst History:

The Restaurant Bristol has a storied past, having hosted luminaries such as President Theodore Roosevelt. As you dine, you become a part of this historical narrative, relishing in the ambiance that has enchanted generations. Every dish carries a touch of elegance, every sip a celebration of culinary mastery.

Musical Interlude:

After your dining experience, embark on a musical journey that transcends time. As you make your way to the iconic Musikverein concert hall, anticipation builds. Settle into the hall that has witnessed countless enchanting performances, each note echoing through its storied walls.

A Symphony of Time and Melody:

As the Vienna Mozart Orchestra takes the stage, you're transported to an era of elegance and refinement. Dressed in historical costumes and wigs, the orchestra performs symphonies and operas from Mozart's timeless repertoire. With every stroke of the conductor's baton, the music of the past comes alive, enveloping the concert hall in a spellbinding aura.

Vienna's Soul in Harmony:

The evening unfolds as a harmonious blend of culinary artistry and musical excellence. From the exquisite flavors of the 3-course dinner to the symphonies that fill the air, each moment is a testament to Vienna's enduring cultural legacy.

As the melodies of Mozart's compositions entwine with the flavors of Austria's finest cuisine, you're transported to a world where elegance, history, and art converge.

Day Trip from Vienna to the Wachau Valley

In the heart of Austria lies a realm of enchantment known as the Wachau Valley, a destination brimming with allure and historical grandeur. Leave the bustling city of Vienna behind as you step into a world where your senses are immersed in charming villages, breathtaking landscapes, and tales of antiquity.

Guided Exploration of Timeless Treasures:

Under the guidance of a knowledgeable expert, your journey unveils treasures beyond imagination. Traverse through the picturesque landscapes, where every turn reveals another facet of Austria's rich heritage. Traveling in a small and intimate group, you'll experience a personalized adventure that ensures every moment is enriched with discovery.

A Rendezvous with History:

As part of this remarkable escapade, you'll explore the UNESCO-listed gems that grace the Wachau Valley. Venture into the medieval embrace of Dürnstein, a town steeped in history and legendary tales. With your guide leading the way, delve into the past as you wander through its cobbled streets and soak in the ambiance that centuries have woven.

Savoring Local Delights:

Amidst this voyage of exploration, take a pause to delight your taste buds with the flavors of the region. At a traditional local wine tavern, relish an authentic lunch that embodies the essence of the Wachau Valley. The opportunity to taste the finest wines of the region is an indulgence not to be missed. In the intimate setting of a charming cellar, immerse yourself in the symphony of flavors that only the Wachau Valley can offer.

A Symphony of Landscapes:

As you traverse the Austrian countryside in the comfort of a well-appointed coach, the landscapes unfold like a masterpiece. Each scene is a stroke of nature's brush, a harmonious blend of rolling hills, vineyards, and the meandering Danube River. Let serenity wash over you as you bask in the tranquil vistas that surround you.

A Dance with the Danube:

For those who embark on this journey between May and September, a Danube River cruise awaits, adding yet another layer of enchantment to your day. Glide along the gentle waters, witnessing the rhythm of life along the riverbanks. Travel from the picturesque village of Spitz to the splendid town of Melk, a voyage that intertwines the beauty of nature with the stories of mankind.

Pedal Through History on a Bike and City Tour

In the heart of Vienna's enchanting streets, a unique adventure beckons—one that combines the freedom of cycling with the guidance of a knowledgeable local. Pedal past the city's most iconic attractions, each one a treasure trove of history and culture. Led by a seasoned guide, this bike and city tour offers an immersive journey through Vienna's tapestry of tales.

A Panoramic Path:

Saddle up and embark on a leisurely ride that weaves through Vienna's storied streets. As your wheels turn, you'll be greeted by the grandeur of the Albertina, the timeless beauty of St. Stephen's Cathedral, and the artistic presence of the Vienna State Opera. Pedal through the serene Stadtpark, a haven of tranquility amidst the urban landscape, and bask in the majesty of Heldenplatz.

Stories Etched in Stone:

While you navigate the bike paths and quieter streets, your guide will regale you with captivating stories that breathe life into each landmark. Behind every facade lies a tale of intrigue, and your guide's insights transform the scenery into a living tableau of Vienna's history. The city's narrative unfolds with every turn of your pedal, adding depth and color to the sights before you.

Morning, Afternoon, or Evening Exploration:

This cycling adventure caters to your schedule and preferences, offering a choice of morning, afternoon, or evening departures. Whether you wish to start your day with the sun's embrace, bask in the afternoon's glow, or witness Vienna's transformation as evening sets in, the choice is yours.

Vienna's Soul on Two Wheels:

The Bike and City Tour of Vienna is not just a ride; it's an immersive encounter with the city's essence. It's a fusion of exploration, education, and adventure—a chance to see Vienna from a fresh perspective while embracing the spirit of discovery. With each pedal, Vienna's stories come to life, inviting you to be a part of its ongoing narrative.

Embark on a Journey from Vienna to Hallstatt

A Seamless Exploration: Small-Group Tour with a Dash of Comfort

Venture beyond Vienna's confines and immerse yourself in the captivating allure of Hallstatt, a gem nestled within Austria's embrace. This full-day odyssey promises a seamless adventure, facilitated by private transportation, allowing you to uncover numerous attractions with time on your side.

Guided Tales and Filming Locations:

Your journey unfolds under the guidance of an informative guide, whose narration paints vivid stories of the landscape passing by. Traverse through more points of interest in less time, thanks to the efficiency of private transportation. As you travel, relish the opportunity to visit filming locations that once set the stage for cinematic classics like 'The Sound of Music' and beyond. Each stop is a testament to the fusion of reality and the silver screen.

Hallstatt:

Upon reaching Hallstatt, embark on a captivating sightseeing tour that unravels the town's tapestry of charm. Your senses will dance amidst the cobblestone streets, historic architecture, and the pristine waters of Lake Hallstatt. As the guided tour concludes, you're bestowed with the gift of free time to explore independently. Wander at your own pace, discover hidden corners, and let the town's enchantment guide your steps.

The Homeward Sojourn:

As the sun sets on your Hallstatt escapade, your return journey is nothing short of comfortable. Reflect upon the day's enchantment as you relax in the private transportation that carries you back to Vienna. With the memories of Hallstatt etched in your heart, the journey home becomes a tranquil moment of reflection and anticipation for future explorations.

A Celebration of Pastries and Delights

A Guided Culinary Expedition: Satisfy Your Cravings with Expert Insight

Vienna, a city steeped in history and culture, has bestowed upon the world a treasure trove of traditional pastries that echo its rich heritage. Immerse yourself in the heart of this confectionery legacy as you embark on a journey that tantalizes your taste buds and enriches your understanding of Vienna's culinary traditions.

Embark on a Sweet Adventure:

In the company of a knowledgeable guide, explore the city's most renowned Viennese bakeries, pastry shops, and chocolatiers. Each establishment is a testament to the artistry and dedication that have crafted Vienna's reputation as a haven for confectionery excellence. As you traverse these delicious havens, you'll partake in delectable tastings that offer a symphony of flavors and textures, each morsel an ode to Vienna's devotion to the sweet side of life.

From Tradition to Innovation:

This journey transcends time, inviting you to savor traditional pastries that have graced Viennese coffee houses for generations. Yet, it also opens the door to contemporary confections that reflect the city's evolution while honoring its culinary heritage. Each bite carries a story of innovation, creativity, and a passion for perfection.

The Expert's Insight:

Your guide, an expert in Vienna's culinary landscape, offers a wealth of knowledge that enriches your tasting experience. As you indulge in the delightful offerings, your guide's insights provide a backdrop to the flavors, allowing you to appreciate the craftsmanship that goes into each creation. Discover the stories behind these sweet masterpieces, and gain a deeper connection to Vienna's food culture.

Satisfy Your Sweet Tooth:

This pastry and dessert food tour is an invitation to relish the delectable treasures that Vienna offers. It's an expedition that tantalizes your senses, enriches your palate, and offers a glimpse into the heart of a city that cherishes its culinary heritage. With each bite, you're not just indulging in desserts—you're immersing yourself in the very essence of Vienna's soul.

Hop-On Hop-Off Freedom

In the heart of Vienna, a world of wonders awaits your discovery. Embark on a journey that allows you to curate your own adventure as you traverse this vibrant city. With a choice of 24, 48, or 72 hours, the hop-on hop-off bus tour grants you the freedom to explore Vienna's top attractions at your own pace, ensuring a personalized experience that suits your every desire.

Vienna's Icons:

From the resplendent Vienna State Opera to the imperial grandeur of Hofburg Palace, from the towering elegance of Danube Tower to the enchanting Schonbrunn Palace, this journey unfolds before you with a panorama of majesty and history. Climb aboard the open-air, double-decker bus, where 360-degree views transform the city into an ever-changing masterpiece.

A Symphony of Choices:

As the bus winds its way through Vienna's streets, you hold the reins of exploration. At any moment, you can choose to disembark and immerse yourself in the allure of a specific attraction. Wander through the grandeur of Hofburg Palace, stand in awe of the Vienna State Opera's opulence, ascend the heights of Danube Tower for breathtaking views, and meander through the splendors of Schonbrunn Palace's gardens.

Freedom to Discover:

The essence of this hop-on hop-off experience lies in the freedom it offers. No longer bound by rigid itineraries, you decide where to linger and where to move on. Whether you're captivated by a historic monument, enticed by a charming street, or simply wish to pause and savor Viennese culture, this journey evolves with your whims.

A Tale of Vienna Unfolds:

The Vienna Hop On Hop Off City Tour is not just a bus ride; it's a symphony of exploration. It's an opportunity to be immersed in Vienna's soul, to uncover its treasures, and to create memories that resonate with your personal tastes and desires. With every hop on and hop off, Vienna's story unfolds before you, inviting you to play an active role in the narrative.

A 3-Hour Journey through Schönbrunn Palace

Beyond the façade of Schönbrunn Palace lies a world of opulence and history waiting to be explored. Step into this realm of magnificence as you embark on a guided tour led by a historian guide. With your small group, comprising only six individuals, you'll delve into the palace's most resplendent chambers, gaining insights that extend far beyond the surface.

40 Rooms of Extravagance:

Together with your guide, you'll traverse approximately 40 of Schönbrunn Palace's most lavishly adorned rooms. As you meander through these opulent spaces, each exuding its own unique charm, you'll come to understand the significance of this architectural masterpiece. With the privilege of a small group, you'll have ample opportunity to absorb the details and intricacies that make each room a chapter in the palace's story.

A Royal Tapestry of History:

As your guide leads you through the palace's hallowed halls, you'll be immersed in the rich history that echoes within these walls. Discover the lives of royals who once called Schönbrunn home, including the enigmatic Franz Joseph. With each step, your guide unravels stories that weave the past into the present, painting a vivid picture of the palace's role in history.

A Symphony of Noteworthy Encounters:

Your journey extends beyond history to embrace cultural significance. Stand in the room where Mozart once graced the palace with his music, and let the echoes of his compositions come alive in your imagination. Behold a secretaire that once belonged to Marie Antoinette, a tangible link to a bygone era of elegance and grace.

Schönbrunn's Essence Unveiled:

The Schönbrunn Palace tour is more than an expedition; it's a voyage into the heart of culture and history. It's an opportunity to understand the palace's significance, to feel the presence of those who once walked its corridors, and to witness the grandeur that defines its existence. With your historian guide as your compass, you'll unveil the unseen layers that make Schönbrunn a masterpiece beyond compare.

The Spanish Riding School Experience

In the heart of Vienna, a world of equestrian artistry beckons. Venture to the renowned Spanish Riding School and immerse yourself in a morning of unparalleled elegance and horsemanship. As you present your ticket, the doors to this storied institution swing open, granting you a privileged view of their legendary Lipizzaner horses in action.

A Dance of Grace and Mastery:

Within the hallowed halls of the Spanish Riding School, a spectacle unfolds that marries grace with mastery—the morning exercise of the revered Lipizzaner horses. These stallions, renowned for their beauty and skill, undergo a training that sets the standard for classical dressage. As you take your place, you become a witness to this dance of equine excellence, a spectacle that transcends mere performance.

Unveiling the Secrets of Equine Artistry:

As you watch the Lipizzaner horses move with precision and elegance, you'll gain insight into the meticulous training that propels them to this pinnacle of mastery. Every movement carries a story of dedication, a testament to the bond forged between rider and horse. Witness the communication that occurs through the slightest of cues, and feel the atmosphere pulsate with a shared language of trust and respect.

An Experience Tailored to You:

The Spanish Riding School offers you the privilege of time. How long you choose to linger and immerse yourself in this experience is entirely at your discretion. The morning exercise unfolds over a span of up to two hours, allowing you to savor each moment of this equine symphony to its fullest.

The Majesty of Equine Mastery:

Witnessing the morning exercise at the Spanish Riding School isn't just an event—it's an encounter with the essence of horsemanship and artistry. It's an opportunity to glimpse into a world where elegance, dedication, and the bond between horse and rider converge. The Lipizzaner horses dance not only for themselves but for those who bear witness, inviting you to be part of a legacy that transcends time.

IMPERIAL PALACES AND SITES

Vienna's imperial history is beautifully reflected in its grand palaces and historic sites. These opulent landmarks offer a glimpse into the city's rich past and the grandeur of the Austro-Hungarian Empire. Here are some of the most iconic imperial palaces and sites you should explore in Vienna:

Schönbrunn Palace (Schloss Schönbrunn)

Schönbrunn Palace, often referred to as Schloss Schönbrunn, is one of Vienna's most iconic and visited landmarks. This magnificent palace and its surrounding gardens hold a significant place in Austrian history and culture. Here's an in-depth look at Schönbrunn Palace:

History and Background:

Originally a hunting lodge, Schönbrunn was transformed into a grand imperial residence during the reign of Emperor Leopold I in the late 17th century. However, it gained its current form and splendor during the reign of Empress Maria Theresa and her successors.

Architecture and Design:

Schönbrunn Palace is a prime example of Baroque architecture, characterized by its symmetrical layout, ornate facades, and opulent interiors. The central building of the palace features a grand central hall, lavishly decorated rooms, and apartments for the imperial family.

Imperial Apartments:

Visitors can explore the elegantly furnished imperial apartments, where the Habsburg emperors and empresses once lived. These rooms offer a glimpse into their daily lives, preferences, and taste.

Gardens and Grounds:

The extensive gardens surrounding Schönbrunn Palace are meticulously landscaped in the French and English styles, offering a serene and picturesque setting. A central feature of the garden is the Glücksbrunn, a monumental fountain adorned with sculptures representing allegorical figures and mythological scenes. Visitors can enjoy the hedge maze and labyrinth, providing fun for all ages.

Gloriette:

Perched on a hill behind the palace, the Gloriette is a triumphal arch-like structure that offers breathtaking panoramic views of Schönbrunn Palace and the city of Vienna.

Historical Significance:

During the Napoleonic Wars, Schönbrunn was occupied by Napoleon Bonaparte, and his quarters can be visited as part of the palace tour.

Sisi Museum:

The Sisi Museum is dedicated to Empress Elisabeth (often known as Sisi), providing insight into her life, her personal belongings, and her impact on Austrian history.

Cultural Events:

Schönbrunn Palace hosts various cultural events, including classical concerts and performances, allowing visitors to experience the palace's grandeur in a musical setting.

UNESCO World Heritage Site:

In 1996, Schönbrunn Palace and its gardens were designated as a UNESCO World Heritage Site, recognizing their historical, cultural, and architectural significance.

Visitor Experience:

Guided tours are available in various languages, providing detailed insights into the history, architecture, and stories behind the palace. Audio guides are also available, allowing visitors to explore at their own pace while learning about the palace's history.

Hofburg Palace

The Hofburg Palace, located in the heart of Vienna, is a historic complex that served as the imperial residence of the Habsburg dynasty for centuries. This sprawling palace is a blend of architectural styles and houses numerous museums, institutions, and landmarks. Here's an in-depth look at the Hofburg Palace:

History and Background:

The Hofburg has been the seat of power for the Habsburg rulers since the 13th century. Over the centuries, it expanded and evolved into a grand complex of buildings.

Architecture and Design:

The Hofburg exhibits a mix of architectural styles due to its expansions and renovations over the centuries. It encompasses elements of Gothic, Renaissance, Baroque, and Neoclassical architecture.

Key Buildings and Areas:

- **Swiss Wing:** The Swiss Wing was originally built as a fortress and later served as the residence for the rulers.

- **Imperial Apartments:** Explore the Imperial Apartments, where Emperor Franz Joseph and Empress Elisabeth (Sisi) once lived. These lavish rooms are adorned with opulent furnishings and décor.

- **Sisi Museum:** The museum is dedicated to Empress Elisabeth, providing insights into her life, personality, and impact on Austrian history.

- **Silver Collection:** This museum showcases a stunning array of dining settings, tableware, and historical objects associated with royal banquets and ceremonies.

Spanish Riding School:

The Spanish Riding School, located within the Hofburg, is famous for its Lipizzaner horses and classical dressage performances. The Winter Riding School hosts these elegant displays.

National Library (Österreichische Nationalbibliothek):

The National Library houses a vast collection of books, manuscripts, and historical artifacts. The State Hall, with its baroque architecture and ceiling frescoes, is a highlight.

Imperial Crypt (Kapuzinergruft):

Beneath the Capuchin Church, the Imperial Crypt is the burial site of Habsburg emperors, empresses, and other royals. The crypt offers insights into the dynasty's history and rituals.

Michaelertrakt:

The Michaelertrakt houses the Hofburg's archaeological museum, showcasing Vienna's ancient past through artifacts and exhibits.

MuseumsQuartier:

The Hofburg's vicinity also includes the MuseumsQuartier, a cultural complex housing various museums, art spaces, cafes, and shops.

Historical Significance:

The Hofburg played a pivotal role during the Congress of Vienna (1814-1815), where European leaders gathered to reshape the continent after the Napoleonic Wars.

Visitor Experience:

Guided tours offer insight into different aspects of the palace's history, architecture, and royal life. Consider purchasing combined tickets that grant access to multiple museums and attractions within the Hofburg complex.

Belvedere Palace (Schloss Belvedere)

Belvedere Palace, commonly referred to as Schloss Belvedere, is a magnificent palace complex in Vienna that stands as a testament to Baroque architecture and artistic splendor. This iconic landmark comprises two palaces, the Upper Belvedere and the Lower Belvedere, along with stunning gardens. Here's a closer look at the Belvedere Palace:

History and Background:

The palace was built in the early 18th century by Prince Eugene of Savoy, a military commander and art patron. Belvedere Palace was intended to be a summer residence and a showcase for Prince Eugene's art collection.

Architecture and Design:

Belvedere Palace is a masterpiece of Baroque architecture, characterized by its ornate facades, elaborate decorations, and dramatic use of light and shadow. The palace complex is known for its symmetrical layout, axial perspectives, and grand staircases.

Upper Belvedere:

- **Art Museum:** The Upper Belvedere houses an impressive art collection, featuring Austrian art from the Middle Ages to the present day.

- **The Kiss:** One of the most famous artworks displayed here is Gustav Klimt's iconic painting "The Kiss," which has become a symbol of Vienna's artistic heritage.

- ❖ **Vienna 1900 Collection:** The museum also showcases works from the Vienna Secession movement and artists like Egon Schiele.

Lower Belvedere:

The Lower Belvedere hosts temporary exhibitions and events, offering a platform for contemporary and historical art.

Palace Gardens:

The palace is surrounded by stunning gardens designed in both French and English styles, offering a serene oasis in the heart of the city. The gardens feature ornamental pools, fountains, and sculptures, enhancing the beauty of the surroundings.

Orangery:

The Belvedere Orangery is a greenhouse complex that was used to protect citrus trees during the winter months. It now hosts events and exhibitions.

Historical Significance:

In 1735, the Treaty of Belvedere was signed here, ending the War of the Polish Succession.

Visitor Experience:

Guided tours are available, providing insights into the history, architecture, and artworks of the palace. Audio guides offer information about the art and history as you explore the palace.

Cultural Events:

Concerts and Performances: The Belvedere Palace hosts cultural events, including classical music concerts and performances in its splendid setting.

UNESCO World Heritage Site:

The Belvedere Palace and Gardens are recognized as a UNESCO World Heritage Site, reflecting their cultural and historical significance.

Schloss Hetzendorf

Schloss Hetzendorf, located in the Hetzendorf district of Vienna, is a lesser-known yet charming palace that holds historical and architectural significance. This palace, characterized by its Rococo architecture and picturesque gardens, offers a glimpse into Vienna's imperial past. Here's an overview of Schloss Hetzendorf:

History and Background:

Hetzendorf was built in the early 18th century as a hunting lodge for the Habsburgs. It was later expanded and transformed into a lavish Rococo palace during the reign of Empress Maria Theresa.

Architecture and Design:

The palace's architecture is a prime example of Rococo style, known for its ornate decorations, pastel colors, and intricate detailing. Schloss Hetzendorf exudes elegance and refinement, showcasing the luxurious tastes of the Habsburg nobility.

Key Features:

The palace features a central building with wings on either side, forming a U-shape around a central courtyard. Elaborate stucco work, gilded decorations, and delicate frescoes adorn the interior spaces.

Imperial Residence:

Empress Maria Theresa used Schloss Hetzendorf as a residence for her daughters. It served as a place for their education, social gatherings, and entertainment.

Orangerie:

The palace's beautiful garden is complemented by an orangerie, a pavilion where citrus trees were protected during the colder months.

Park and Gardens:

The palace is surrounded by picturesque gardens that reflect the Rococo aesthetic with their symmetry and ornate landscaping. The gardens feature fountains, statues, and manicured hedges, typical of Baroque and Rococo garden design.

Today:

In the 20th century, Schloss Hetzendorf became the location of the Fashion School of the Vienna Chamber of Commerce and Industry (Modeschule der WKW).

Visitor Experience:

Guided tours may be available to explore the palace's history, architecture, and the roles it played during the Habsburg era. Occasionally, cultural events, exhibitions, and workshops are hosted within the palace.

Imperial Crypt (Kapuzinergruft)

The Imperial Crypt, known as Kapuzinergruft in German, is a historic burial site located beneath the Capuchin Church in Vienna. This crypt is the final resting place for many members of the Habsburg dynasty, including emperors, empresses, and other prominent figures. Here's more information about the Imperial Crypt:

Historical Significance:

The Imperial Crypt has been the principal burial site for members of the Habsburg family since its establishment in the 17th century. The crypt serves as a testament to the power and legacy of the Habsburg dynasty, one of the most influential royal families in European history.

Architecture and Layout:

The crypt is located below the Capuchin Church. It consists of a series of underground chambers and vaults, each dedicated to different members of the Habsburg family.

Burials and Tombs:

Many emperors, empresses, archdukes, archduchesses, and other notable figures are interred here, including Maria Theresa and Emperor Franz Joseph I. Elaborate tombs, sarcophagi, and memorial plaques commemorate the lives and achievements of those buried here.

Kapuzinerkirche (Capuchin Church):

The crypt is accessed through the Capuchin Church, which has close ties to the Habsburgs. The church itself is known for its elegant Baroque architecture.

Historical Exhibits:

The Imperial Crypt is open to the public, and visitors can explore the various chambers and learn about the history of the Habsburg dynasty through informative displays. The exhibits provide insights into the elaborate funeral rituals and dynastic traditions observed by the Habsburgs.

Unique Experience:

Visiting the Imperial Crypt offers a unique opportunity to reflect on the rich history of the Habsburg monarchy and their impact on European history.

Opening Hours:

The Imperial Crypt has specific opening hours, so it's advisable to check the official website or local sources for the most current information.

Guided Tours:

Guided tours may be available to provide in-depth information about the crypt's history, the individuals buried there, and the significance of their legacy.

The Vienna Residence Orchestra

The Vienna Residence Orchestra is a renowned musical ensemble that specializes in performing classical music in Vienna, the city often referred to as the "City of Music." This orchestra offers visitors a unique opportunity to experience the enchanting melodies of Austrian classical music in the heart of Vienna. Here's more about the Vienna Residence Orchestra:

Overview:

The Vienna Residence Orchestra is a chamber music ensemble dedicated to performing the works of renowned composers such as Wolfgang Amadeus Mozart and Johann Strauss II.

Venue:

Performances by the Vienna Residence Orchestra often take place in historic and opulent venues that resonate with Vienna's musical heritage. These venues may include palaces, concert halls, or historical buildings.

Repertoire:

The orchestra's repertoire typically focuses on Viennese classical music, capturing the essence of the city's rich musical tradition. Audiences can expect to hear compositions by Mozart, Strauss, and other composers who have shaped Vienna's musical legacy.

Concert Experience:

The Vienna Residence Orchestra offers orchestral performances that include a variety of classical compositions, waltzes, polkas, and operatic selections. The ensemble size may vary, but it generally features a chamber orchestra with musicians specializing in different instruments.

Cultural Experience:

Attending a performance by the Vienna Residence Orchestra offers a chance to immerse oneself in the authentic Viennese musical ambiance. The orchestra strives to recreate the spirit of Vienna's historic musical culture, which was deeply woven into the fabric of the city's society.

Concert Schedule:

The Vienna Residence Orchestra may have scheduled performances throughout the year, allowing visitors to enjoy classical music during various seasons.

Audience Interaction:

Some performances by the Vienna Residence Orchestra may include opportunities for audience members to participate by dancing or clapping along during certain pieces.

Ticket Information:

It's advisable to book tickets for performances by the Vienna Residence Orchestra in advance, as these events can be popular among both tourists and locals.

Cultural Enrichment:

Attending a performance by the Vienna Residence Orchestra can be a wonderful way to engage with Vienna's cultural heritage and musical legacy.

Apothecary Museum of the Vienna General Hospital

The Apothecary Museum of the Vienna General Hospital, known as "Apothekenmuseum im Allgemeinen Krankenhaus" in German, offers a fascinating glimpse into the history of medicine and pharmacy practices. Located within the historic Vienna General Hospital, this museum showcases an extensive collection of pharmaceutical artifacts, tools, and equipment, providing insights into the evolution of medical practices over the centuries. Here's what you can expect from a visit to the Apothecary Museum:

Historical Significance:

The Vienna General Hospital, founded in 1784, has a long history of providing medical care to the people of Vienna. The Apothecary Museum reflects the hospital's role in healthcare and its contributions to medical advancements.

Collection and Exhibits:

The museum features an impressive array of pharmaceutical tools, equipment, and artifacts dating back to different eras. Explore the history of medicine preparation, from herbal remedies to early chemical processes.

Antique Pharmacy Interior:

One of the highlights of the museum is a beautifully restored antique pharmacy interior, showcasing how pharmacies were traditionally organized and decorated.

Medical Knowledge and Practices:

Learn how medical knowledge and practices have evolved over time, shedding light on the challenges and breakthroughs in the field of healthcare.

Historical Context:

The Apothecary Museum provides historical context to medical practices, allowing visitors to understand the medical challenges and solutions of different eras.

Connection to Vienna:

The museum's exhibits offer a connection to Vienna's medical and cultural history, showcasing the role of the hospital in the city's development.

Guided Tours:

Guided tours may be available to offer in-depth information about the artifacts, their significance, and the museum's role in preserving medical history.

Interpretive Displays:

Interactive and informative displays help visitors grasp the complexities of pharmacy and medical practices.

Cultural Heritage:

The Apothecary Museum contributes to Vienna's rich cultural heritage by offering insights into the medical practices and advancements that have shaped the city.

Location:

The museum is located within the Vienna General Hospital complex, making it accessible to both visitors and those interested in medical history.

Opening Hours:

Check the official website or local sources for the most up-to-date information about opening hours and visiting guidelines.

Kaisergruft (Imperial Burial Vault)

The Kaisergruft, also known as the Imperial Burial Vault or Capuchin Crypt, is a historic burial site located beneath the Capuchin Church in Vienna. This crypt serves as the final resting place for numerous members of the Habsburg dynasty, including emperors, empresses, and other notable figures. Here's what you should know about the Kaisergruft:

Habsburg Dynasty:

The Kaisergruft has been the primary burial site for members of the Habsburg family since the 17th century, making it a significant repository of Austrian imperial history.

Underground Crypt:

The Kaisergruft is an underground crypt consisting of several chambers and vaults, each housing the tombs of different Habsburg family members.

Baroque Influences:

The architecture of the crypt reflects the Baroque style, which was prevalent during the period when it was established.

Burials and Tombs:

Many emperors, empresses, archdukes, and archduchesses are interred in the Kaisergruft, making it a place of great historical and dynastic importance. The tombs and memorials are often ornate, reflecting the status and significance of the individuals buried there.

Capuchin Church:

Religious Connection: The Kaisergruft is accessed through the Capuchin Church (Kapuzinerkirche), which is closely associated with the Habsburgs and serves as the public entrance to the crypt.

Cultural and Historical Experience:

Visiting the Kaisergruft provides a unique opportunity to witness the dynastic traditions of the Habsburg family and their impact on European history. The crypt's exhibits offer insights into the lives, reigns, and achievements of the Habsburg rulers.

Opening Hours:

The Kaisergruft has specific opening hours, which can vary depending on the time of year. It's recommended to check the official website or local sources for accurate information.

Guided Tours:

Guided tours may be available, providing historical context and details about the individuals interred in the crypt.

Sensitivity and Respect:

Cultural Sensitivity: Given the solemn and reverent nature of the site, visitors are encouraged to approach the Kaisergruft with respect and consideration.

Note on Timing:

Planning Ahead: When planning a visit, consider checking the crypt's opening hours and any potential closures due to maintenance or special events.

MUSEUM AND GALLERIES

Vienna is a city rich in history, culture, and art, making it a perfect destination for those interested in exploring museums and galleries. Here's a guide to some of the must-visit museums and galleries in Vienna in 2023 and beyond:

Belvedere Palace and Museum

The Belvedere Palace and Museum is a prominent cultural attraction in Vienna, Austria. Comprising two magnificent Baroque palaces, the Upper and Lower Belvedere, along with expansive gardens, this complex is renowned for its stunning architecture, its impressive collection of art, and its historical significance. Here's what you can expect when visiting the Belvedere Palace and Museum:

Collection Highlights:

The Upper Belvedere is home to an exceptional collection of Austrian art from the 19th and 20th centuries. This includes the world's largest collection of works by Gustav Klimt, including his renowned masterpiece "The Kiss." You'll also find works by Egon Schiele, Oskar Kokoschka, and other prominent artists of the Viennese Secession movement.

Palace Architecture:

The Upper Belvedere is a splendid Baroque palace with opulent interiors and breathtaking views of the surrounding city. Its ornate design and elaborate decoration make it a sight to behold both inside and out.

The Kiss:

Gustav Klimt's iconic painting "The Kiss" is one of the most famous artworks in the world. It's a symbol of Viennese art nouveau and is showcased prominently within the Upper Belvedere.

Exhibitions:

The Lower Belvedere features a mix of temporary exhibitions that explore various themes and art forms. From contemporary art to historical retrospectives, the Lower Belvedere offers diverse and thought-provoking exhibitions.

Palace Stables:

The Palace Stables house the Belvedere's collection of medieval art and decorative arts. The stables' architecture itself is impressive, and the collection includes sculptures, armor, and other artifacts.

Belvedere Gardens

The beautifully landscaped gardens between the Upper and Lower Belvedere are a sight to behold, featuring fountains, sculptures, and perfectly manicured green spaces. They provide a serene and picturesque setting for visitors to explore and enjoy.

Visitor Information:

- **Location:** Prinz Eugen-Straße 27, 1030 Vienna, Austria
- **Opening Hours:** The opening hours can vary, so it's advisable to check the official website for the most up-to-date information.

- ❖ **Tickets:** Admission fees apply, and there are various ticket options available, including combination tickets for the Upper and Lower Belvedere.

- ❖ **Guided Tours:** Guided tours are available for both palaces, providing insights into the history, art, and architecture of the complex.

Albertina Museum and Art Gallery

The Albertina Museum and Art Gallery is another cultural gem in Vienna that art enthusiasts shouldn't miss. Located in the heart of the city, this museum is known for its extensive collection of graphic art, spanning from the Renaissance to the present day. Here's what you can expect when visiting the Albertina:

Graphic Art:

The Albertina is renowned for its unparalleled collection of graphic art, which includes drawings, prints, and watercolors. You'll find works by masters like Leonardo da Vinci, Michelangelo, Dürer, Rembrandt, and many more. This collection provides insights into the evolution of artistic techniques and styles over the centuries.

Impressionist and Modern Art:

In addition to its graphic art collection, the Albertina also features a notable collection of Impressionist and Modernist paintings, including works by Monet, Renoir, Picasso, and

Klimt. These paintings offer a diverse range of artistic styles and movements.

Architecture and Sculpture:

The museum's holdings extend to architecture and sculpture, showcasing models, plans, and architectural drawings from various periods.

Exhibitions and Special Events:

The Albertina regularly hosts temporary exhibitions that delve into specific artists, artistic movements, or thematic subjects. These exhibitions provide visitors with fresh perspectives and the opportunity to explore different facets of art history and contemporary art.

Architecture and Location:

The Albertina itself is housed within a historic palace that boasts elegant architecture and a beautiful interior. It's located near other cultural landmarks, making it a convenient stop for those exploring Vienna's cultural offerings.

Visitor Information:

- **Location:** Albertinaplatz 1, 1010 Vienna, Austria
- **Opening Hours:** The opening hours can vary, so it's advisable to check the official website for the most up-to-date information.

- ❖ **Tickets:** Admission fees apply, and there are various ticket options available, including combination tickets for permanent and temporary exhibitions.

- ❖ **Guided Tours:** Guided tours are available for different parts of the museum, providing insights into the collection and its history.

Leopold Museum

The Leopold Museum is a prominent art museum in Vienna, Austria, dedicated to Austrian modern art from the late 19th century to the present day. The museum is named after its founder, Rudolf Leopold, who amassed an impressive collection of artworks that reflect the evolution of Austrian art during this period. Here's what you can expect when visiting the Leopold Museum:

Egon Schiele:

The museum houses the world's largest collection of works by the Austrian Expressionist artist Egon Schiele. You'll find a comprehensive selection of his drawings, watercolors, and paintings, providing insights into his distinctive style and artistic development.

Gustav Klimt:

The Leopold Museum also features works by Gustav Klimt, including several of his iconic pieces. While not as extensive as the collection at the Belvedere, the museum offers a unique perspective on Klimt's contributions to Austrian art.

Viennese Secession and Expressionism:

The museum's collection includes pieces from the Viennese Secession movement and other Austrian Expressionist artists, giving visitors a broader understanding of the artistic movements that shaped the country's cultural landscape.

Design and Applied Arts:

In addition to paintings and drawings, the Leopold Museum showcases design and applied arts, offering insights into the aesthetics and craftsmanship of the era. This includes furniture, glassware, textiles, and more.

Temporary Exhibitions and Events:

The museum hosts temporary exhibitions that explore various themes, artistic movements, and contemporary art practices. These exhibitions provide visitors with opportunities to engage with current artistic trends and diverse perspectives.

Museum Architecture:

The Leopold Museum is housed in a modern building designed by architects Laurids and Manfred Ortner. The architecture complements the museum's collection, providing a contemporary backdrop for the historic and modern artworks.

Visitor Information:

- **Location:** Museumsplatz 1, 1070 Vienna, Austria

- **Opening Hours:** The opening hours can vary, so it's advisable to check the official website for the most up-to-date information.

- **Tickets:** Admission fees apply, and there are various ticket options available, including combination tickets for the Leopold Museum and other museums in the MuseumsQuartier complex.

- **Guided Tours:** Guided tours are available, providing insights into the museum's collection and its significance in the context of Austrian art history.

Kunsthistorisches Museum (Museum of Art History)

The Kunsthistorisches Museum, often referred to as the Museum of Art History, is one of Vienna's most iconic and prestigious cultural institutions. Established in 1891, this museum is renowned for its remarkable collection of European art and historical artifacts, spanning from ancient times to the Baroque period. Here's what you can expect when visiting the Kunsthistorisches Museum:

Paintings:

The museum houses an extensive collection of paintings by some of the most celebrated European artists. Works by artists such as Titian, Caravaggio, Vermeer, and Raphael are on display. The collection includes masterpieces like Vermeer's "The Art of Painting" and Bruegel's "The Tower of Babel."

Sculptures:

The museum's sculpture collection features magnificent pieces from ancient Greece and Rome, as well as sculptures from the Renaissance and Baroque periods. These sculptures provide insights into the evolution of artistic techniques and styles over the centuries.

Decorative Arts:

The Kunsthistorisches Museum also boasts a rich collection of decorative arts, including exquisite furniture, tapestries, porcelain, and armor. These pieces showcase the opulence and craftsmanship of various eras.

Egyptian and Near Eastern Collection:

Explore artifacts from ancient Egypt, the Near East, and the Mediterranean. Marvel at mummies, intricate jewelry, and other artifacts that offer a glimpse into the cultures of these regions.

Coin Cabinet:

The museum is home to one of the world's most impressive coin collections, featuring coins and currency from different historical periods and regions.

Architecture:

The Kunsthistorisches Museum itself is a masterpiece of architecture, designed in the Renaissance Revival style by architect Gottfried Semper. The grand façade, ornate interiors, and elegant marble staircases contribute to the museum's allure.

Special Exhibitions and Events:

In addition to its permanent collection, the museum hosts temporary exhibitions, lectures, workshops, and cultural events throughout the year. These exhibitions often explore specific artists, themes, or historical periods, offering visitors a chance to experience a diverse range of art and culture.

Visitor Information:

- **Location:** Maria-Theresien-Platz, 1010 Vienna, Austria

- ❖ **Opening Hours:** The museum's opening hours can vary, so it's recommended to check the official website for the most up-to-date information.

- ❖ **Tickets:** Admission fees apply, and there are various ticket options available, including combination tickets for multiple museums within the complex.

- ❖ **Guided Tours:** Guided tours in various languages are available, providing insights into the museum's history and collection.

MAK - Austrian Museum of Applied Arts/Contemporary Art

The MAK - Austrian Museum of Applied Arts/Contemporary Art, often referred to simply as the MAK, is a unique cultural institution in Vienna that focuses on applied arts, design, and contemporary art. The museum's diverse collection showcases the intersection of art, design, and everyday life, offering insights into the evolution of aesthetics, craftsmanship, and societal changes. Here's what you can expect when visiting the MAK:

Applied Arts:

The MAK's collection covers a wide range of applied arts, including furniture, textiles, ceramics, glass, and metalwork. You'll find historical pieces that reflect various artistic styles and design movements.

Design:

The museum showcases innovative design objects from different eras, highlighting the evolution of industrial design, graphic design, and architectural design.

Contemporary Art:

In addition to its emphasis on applied arts, the MAK also features contemporary art exhibitions that explore current artistic practices, trends, and socio-cultural themes.

Thematic Exhibitions:

The MAK often hosts thematic exhibitions that delve into specific topics related to design, architecture, and contemporary art. These exhibitions provide visitors with thought-provoking insights into the relationship between art and society.

Vienna Biennale:

The MAK is one of the key institutions that contributes to the Vienna Biennale, a collaborative event that showcases innovative ideas and projects in the fields of art, design, and architecture. The Biennale explores pressing global challenges and future possibilities.

MAK Design Shop:

The museum has a design shop where visitors can purchase unique design objects, books, and other items that reflect the museum's focus on applied arts and contemporary design.

Visitor Information:

- **Location:** Stubenring 5, 1010 Vienna, Austria

- **Opening Hours:** The opening hours can vary, so it's recommended to check the official website for the most up-to-date information.

- **Tickets:** Admission fees apply, and there are various ticket options available. Some exhibitions might have separate entry fees.

- **Guided Tours:** Guided tours and workshops are available, providing insights into the museum's collection and its relevance in the context of design and art history.

MuseumQuartier (MQ)

The MuseumQuartier, often abbreviated as MQ, is a vibrant cultural complex located in the heart of Vienna. It's one of the largest cultural districts in the world and a hub for contemporary art, museums, galleries, performance spaces, and various cultural institutions. The combination of historical architecture and modern art makes it a dynamic and unique destination for both locals and visitors. Here's what you can explore in the MuseumQuartier:

Museums and Galleries:

The MuseumQuartier houses several prominent museums and galleries, including:

- **Leopold Museum:** Dedicated to Austrian modern art, the Leopold Museum features works by artists like Egon Schiele and Gustav Klimt.

- **MUMOK (Museum of Modern Art):** This museum focuses on modern and contemporary art, featuring a diverse range of artistic styles and movements.

- **Kunsthalle Wien:** A contemporary art exhibition space that hosts rotating exhibitions, showcasing works by emerging and established artists.

- **Architekturzentrum Wien (Az W):** Dedicated to architecture and urban planning, this museum explores the development of the built environment.

- **Ludwig Foundation Vienna:** An institution that promotes contemporary art and hosts exhibitions that push the boundaries of artistic expression.

Courtyards:

The spacious courtyards of the MuseumQuartier are popular gathering spots where people can relax, socialize, and enjoy outdoor events.

MQ Libelle:

A distinctive glass and steel structure that provides shade and shelter to visitors, creating a unique architectural feature within the complex.

Events:

The MuseumQuartier hosts a variety of events, including music festivals, open-air cinema screenings, art installations, workshops, and performances. The atmosphere is lively and festive, especially during warmer months.

Cafés and Restaurants:

There are several cafés, bars, and restaurants within the MuseumQuartier where you can enjoy refreshments, meals, and Vienna's coffeehouse culture.

Visitor Information:

- **Location:** Museumsplatz 1, 1070 Vienna, Austria

- **Opening Hours:** Opening hours for the individual museums, galleries, and spaces can vary. It's recommended to check the official website or the respective venues for up-to-date information.

- **Tickets:** Each museum and gallery within the MuseumQuartier has its own admission fees and ticketing options.

- **Guided Tours:** Some museums offer guided tours that provide insights into the exhibitions and the history of the cultural complex.

Secession Building

The Secession Building, also known as the Wiener Secession, is an iconic architectural masterpiece and an important symbol of Vienna's avant-garde art movement. It was built to house exhibitions by the Vienna Secession, a group of artists who rebelled against traditional art norms and sought to create a new artistic language. The building itself is a work of art and is located in the heart of Vienna. Here's what you can learn and experience when visiting the Secession Building:

Architectural Significance:

The Secession Building was designed by architect Joseph Maria Olbrich and completed in 1898. It represents the Jugendstil style, also known as Vienna Art Nouveau, characterized by its decorative and organic forms. The most distinctive feature of the building is its golden dome, covered in intricate ornamental patterns. Atop the dome stands a gilded statue called the "Golden Cabbage," which has become a symbol of the Secession movement.

Beethoven Frieze:

One of the main attractions inside the Secession Building is the famous Beethoven Frieze, a monumental artwork created by Gustav Klimt for the 14th Vienna Secessionist exhibition in 1902. The frieze celebrates the composer Ludwig van Beethoven and embodies themes of human aspiration, suffering, and enlightenment. The Beethoven Frieze is a long, sweeping mural that adorns three walls of a specially designed room within the building. It's a masterpiece of Symbolism and Art Nouveau, and its intricate symbolism and rich colors are a sight to behold.

Secession Movement:

The Vienna Secession was a progressive group of artists who aimed to break away from academic art conventions. The movement emphasized individual expression, innovation, and pushing the boundaries of artistic forms. The Secession Building served as a platform for the Vienna Secessionists to exhibit their works and engage in artistic discourse. The exhibitions held here were instrumental in promoting modern art and shaping Vienna's artistic landscape.

Exhibitions and Events:

The Secession Building continues to host contemporary art exhibitions and events that reflect the spirit of the Secession movement. These exhibitions often feature contemporary artists who challenge traditional norms and explore innovative artistic approaches.

Visitor Information:

- ❖ **Location:** Friedrichstraße 12, 1010 Vienna, Austria

- **Opening Hours:** The opening hours can vary, so it's recommended to check the official website for the most up-to-date information.

- **Tickets:** Admission fees apply for some exhibitions and events. The Beethoven Frieze is a separate attraction within the Secession Building.

Vienna State Opera Museum

The Vienna State Opera Museum, also known as the Wiener Staatsoper Museum, provides visitors with insights into the rich history and cultural significance of the Vienna State Opera, one of the world's most renowned opera houses. The museum offers a glimpse into the world of opera, showcasing the art, music, costumes, and historical context that have shaped the opera's legacy. Here's what you can explore when visiting the Vienna State Opera Museum:

History of the Opera House:

Learn about the history and architecture of the Vienna State Opera, which was inaugurated in 1869. The museum provides information about the building's design, renovations, and the events that have taken place within its walls.

Costumes and Props:

The museum features a collection of costumes, accessories, and props used in various opera productions. These items give visitors a sense of the elaborate costumes and stage design that contribute to the magic of opera performances.

Portraits and Memorabilia:

Discover portraits of famous opera composers, conductors, singers, and other key figures associated with the Vienna State Opera. Explore memorabilia related to significant events in the opera house's history.

Historical Artifacts:

The museum showcases historical artifacts such as programs, posters, and playbills from past opera seasons, offering insights into the operatic repertoire and the performances that captivated audiences throughout the years.

Interactive Experiences:

Engage with interactive displays that allow you to explore the opera's history, productions, and music in an engaging and immersive way.

Vienna Philharmonic Orchestra:

Learn about the Vienna Philharmonic Orchestra's close relationship with the Vienna State Opera and its contributions to the opera's musical excellence.

Visitor Information:

- ❖ **Location**: Opernring 2, 1010 Vienna, Austria

- **Opening Hours:** The opening hours can vary depending on the opera schedule and events. It's advisable to check the official website for the most up-to-date information.

- **Tickets:** Admission fees may apply, and there might be separate fees for special exhibitions or guided tours.

- **Guided Tours:** Guided tours of the Vienna State Opera might include visits to the museum, the auditorium, and other areas of the opera house.

Ludwig Foundation Vienna

The Ludwig Foundation Vienna, also known as the Ludwig Foundation for Art and Science, is an institution that focuses on promoting contemporary art and supporting cultural initiatives in Vienna, Austria. It is part of the international network of Ludwig Foundations, which were established by art collectors Irene and Peter Ludwig to foster the arts and cultural exchange. Here's an overview of what the Ludwig Foundation Vienna is about:

Supporting Contemporary Art:

The foundation plays a key role in supporting contemporary artists, exhibitions, and cultural projects. It often collaborates with artists, curators, and cultural institutions to create exhibitions that reflect the current artistic landscape and challenge traditional boundaries.

Exhibitions and Cultural Events:

The Ludwig Foundation Vienna organizes exhibitions, events, and projects that showcase innovative and experimental contemporary art. These exhibitions provide a platform for artists to present their work and engage with diverse audiences.

Cultural Exchange and Dialogue:

The foundation aims to facilitate cultural exchange and dialogue by bringing together artists, curators, scholars, and the public. Through its programs, it encourages discussions on art, culture, and society.

Educational Initiatives:

The foundation often incorporates educational components into its exhibitions and programs, engaging audiences of all ages and backgrounds in conversations about contemporary art.

Supporting Emerging Artists:

The Ludwig Foundation Vienna is known for its commitment to nurturing emerging artists and providing them with opportunities to showcase their work. This support helps to foster the growth of new talents in the contemporary art scene.

Visitor Information:

The Ludwig Foundation Vienna might not have a specific physical location, as it operates through collaborations, exhibitions, and projects across various venues in Vienna. When the foundation hosts exhibitions or events, information about the specific location, dates, and details will be available through their official website and promotional materials.

ARCHITECTURAL MARVELS

Vienna is a city renowned for its stunning architectural heritage, which spans centuries and includes a diverse array of styles. Here are some of the architectural marvels you shouldn't miss when exploring Vienna:

St. Stephen's Cathedral (Stephansdom)

St. Stephen's Cathedral, commonly known as Stephansdom, is one of Vienna's most iconic landmarks and a symbol of the city. This Gothic masterpiece is renowned for its stunning architecture, rich history, and cultural significance. Here's what you need to know about St. Stephen's Cathedral:

Architecture and Design:

St. Stephen's Cathedral is a prime example of Gothic architecture, characterized by its pointed arches, ribbed vaults, and intricate stone carvings. The cathedral features a distinctive diamond-patterned tile roof, a landmark visible from many parts of Vienna. The South Tower, known as the "Steffl," stands at 136 meters (446 feet) and offers panoramic views of Vienna. Climbing to the top is a popular activity for visitors.

History:

The cathedral's origins date back to the 12th century when it was constructed on the site of earlier churches. Over the centuries, it underwent numerous expansions, renovations, and modifications.

St. Stephen's Cathedral played a significant role in Vienna's history, witnessing important events such as weddings, funerals, and coronations of Austrian royalty.

Interior:

The interior of the cathedral is equally impressive, featuring a nave with towering columns, beautiful stained glass windows, and intricate stone carvings. The High Altar, a masterpiece of Baroque art, is a focal point within the cathedral. It showcases intricate sculptures and decorative elements.

Pummerin Bell:

The Pummerin, one of the largest bells in Europe, is housed in the North Tower. It was cast in the 18th century and has become a symbol of resilience for the city. It tolls on special occasions and significant events.

Catacombs and Treasure:

Visitors to St. Stephen's Cathedral can explore the catacombs beneath the church, where numerous members of the Habsburg royal family and other notable figures are buried. The cathedral also houses a Treasury (Schatzkammer) that contains valuable religious artifacts, including medieval sculptures, vestments, and religious relics.

Events and Services:

St. Stephen's Cathedral is an active place of worship. Regular masses, concerts, and special religious services are held here. The cathedral also hosts musical events, including organ recitals and choral performances.

Visiting Tips:

- Entry to the cathedral is usually free, but certain areas such as the catacombs, the South Tower, and the Treasure require separate admission fees.

- Climbing the South Tower involves a steep ascent, so be prepared for some physical exertion.

- Dress modestly when visiting the cathedral, as it is a place of worship.

Vienna State Opera (Wiener Staatsoper)

The Vienna State Opera, known as the Wiener Staatsoper in German, is one of the most prestigious and renowned opera houses in the world. Situated in the heart of Vienna, the opera house has a storied history, exceptional acoustics, and an illustrious roster of performances. Here's everything you need to know about the Vienna State Opera:

History:

The Vienna State Opera was inaugurated in 1869 under Emperor Franz Joseph I. It replaced the old court opera house and quickly established itself as a cultural hub for classical music and opera. Over the years, the opera house has been a venue for world premieres of numerous operas by renowned composers, adding to its historical significance.

Architecture and Design:

The Vienna State Opera features an opulent neo-Renaissance architectural style, designed by architects August Sicard von Sicardsburg and Eduard van der Nüll. The grand exterior is adorned with sculptures and intricate details, showcasing the elegance and magnificence of the building.

Acoustics and Performance Spaces:

The opera house is celebrated for its excellent acoustics, which contribute to the unparalleled experience of the performances. The main auditorium boasts seating for over 2,000 spectators, providing a sense of intimacy despite its grand size. The stage is equipped with advanced technology to accommodate elaborate sets, lighting effects, and intricate productions.

Repertoire and Performances:

The Vienna State Opera offers a diverse repertoire that covers a wide range of operatic works, from classic masterpieces by Mozart, Verdi, and Wagner to contemporary compositions. The opera house hosts regular opera performances, ballets, and occasionally concerts, ensuring a dynamic calendar of events.

Standing Room Tickets:

The Vienna State Opera is known for its standing room tickets (Stehplätze), which allow budget-conscious visitors to enjoy world-class performances at a fraction of the price. These tickets offer access to designated standing areas in the upper levels of the auditorium.

Tours and Museum:

Visitors interested in the opera house's history and behind-the-scenes operations can take guided tours that provide insights into the architecture, production, and daily life of the opera house. The opera house also features a museum where you can learn about its history, famous artists, and opera-related artifacts.

Dress Code:

While there isn't a strict dress code, many patrons choose to dress elegantly when attending performances at the Vienna State Opera. Formal attire is common, but attire varies among the audience.

Season and Schedule:

The opera house's performance schedule usually runs from September to June, with a break during the summer months. To secure tickets for popular performances, it's advisable to book in advance, especially for premieres and special events.

Hundertwasserhaus

Hundertwasserhaus is an architectural gem located in Vienna that stands out for its unique and whimsical design. Designed by the Austrian artist and architect Friedensreich Hundertwasser, the building is a prime example of his distinctive style, characterized by vibrant colors, irregular shapes, and a harmony with nature. Here's what you need to know about the Hundertwasserhaus:

Architecture and Design:

The Hundertwasserhaus was completed in 1985 as an apartment building with a total of 52 apartments. The building features uneven floors, undulating lines, colorful mosaics, and a variety of materials such as ceramic tiles, glass fragments, and ornate ironwork. Hundertwasser's philosophy of "architecture in harmony with nature" is evident in the inclusion of trees and vegetation on the balconies and roofs, creating a sense of living in a garden.

Philosophy and Inspiration:

Friedensreich Hundertwasser was known for his rejection of the rigid geometry of modern architecture and his emphasis on organic forms, natural materials, and individuality. The building reflects his vision of architecture that celebrates individual creativity and coexistence with nature, embracing what he called "tree tenants" and "window rights."

Colorful Façade:

The exterior of the Hundertwasserhaus is adorned with a vibrant array of colors, geometric patterns, and mosaics. No two windows are the same, each displaying its own color scheme and design.

Public Access:

While the Hundertwasserhaus is a residential building, visitors can admire the exterior and the unique architecture from the street. The building has become a popular attraction for tourists interested in art and architecture.

Kunst Haus Wien:

Hundertwasser's influence extends beyond the Hundertwasserhaus. Kunst Haus Wien, located nearby, is a museum dedicated to his work and artistic philosophy. It features exhibitions of his paintings, graphics, and architectural designs.

Souvenirs and Shops:

The surrounding area offers shops where you can purchase items inspired by Hundertwasser's art, including prints, postcards, and other memorabilia.

Visiting Tips:

- ❖ Since the Hundertwasserhaus is a residential building, it's important to be respectful of the residents' privacy when visiting.

- ❖ The building's exterior is easily accessible for photos and admiration, even if you don't enter the apartments.

Austrian Parliament Building (Parlament)

The Austrian Parliament Building, known as the Parlament, is an impressive neoclassical structure located in Vienna. It serves as the meeting place for the two houses of the Austrian Parliament, the National Council and the Federal Council. The building's grand architecture and historical significance make it a notable landmark in the city. Here's what you should know about the Austrian Parliament Building:

Architecture and Design:

Designed by architect Theophil Hansen, the Parliament Building was constructed between 1874 and 1883 in the neoclassical style, characterized by its symmetry, columns, and pediments. The building's facade is adorned with Corinthian columns and sculptures that represent various allegorical figures, symbolizing concepts such as wisdom, justice, and strength.

Pallas Athena Fountain:

In front of the Parliament Building stands the Pallas Athena Fountain, a sculptural masterpiece designed by Carl Kundmann. The central figure represents Athena, the Greek goddess of wisdom and courage.

Interior:

The interior of the Parliament Building features elegant and ornate halls, including the Federal Council Chamber and the National Council Chamber. The Pallas Athena Hall, an opulent ceremonial hall, is often used for special events and official ceremonies.

Sessions and Visits:

The Austrian Parliament holds sessions and debates on legislative matters within the building. Some of these sessions are open to the public, providing insight into the country's political processes. Guided tours are available for visitors who want to learn more about the history, architecture, and functioning of the Austrian Parliament.

Democracy and Symbolism:

The Parliament Building represents Austria's commitment to democracy and is a symbol of the nation's legislative power and governance. The architecture and design of the building emphasize democratic ideals and civic virtues, reflecting the importance of democratic governance in Austrian society.

Visiting Tips:

❖ Check the official website for information on guided tours and visiting hours.

❖ If you're interested in observing parliamentary sessions, it's a good idea to plan your visit accordingly and check the schedule in advance.

❖ The Parliament Building is located near other notable landmarks, such as the Hofburg Palace and Vienna City Hall, making it a convenient stop for sightseeing.

Karlskirche (St. Charles's Church)

Karlskirche, also known as St. Charles's Church, is a magnificent Baroque church located in Vienna. Designed by the architect Johann Bernhard Fischer von Erlach and completed in the early 18th century, the church stands as a stunning example of Baroque architecture and is one of Vienna's most recognizable landmarks. Here's what you need to know about Karlskirche:

Architecture and Design:

Karlskirche is renowned for its impressive Baroque architecture, characterized by its dramatic domed structure, intricate details, and elaborate decorative elements. The facade of the church is flanked by two large columns topped with sculptures. The central entrance is adorned with a monumental triangular pediment. The dome is a striking feature of Karlskirche. It combines elements of both Roman and Greek architecture, creating a harmonious and visually captivating composition.

Interior:

The interior of Karlskirche is equally stunning, with opulent decor, marble columns, and ornate frescoes. The high altar features a painting depicting St. Charles Borromeo, the patron saint of the church, surrounded by angels.

Frescoes and Art:

The frescoes inside the dome are the work of the famous Baroque artist Johann Michael Rottmayr. They depict scenes from the life of St. Charles Borromeo, as well as allegorical figures representing various virtues.

Viewing Platform:

One of the unique features of Karlskirche is the opportunity to ascend a platform inside the dome, allowing visitors to get a close look at the frescoes and a panoramic view of the interior.

Accessibility:

The viewing platform is accessible via an elevator, making it possible for visitors to enjoy the intricate details of the dome's interior without climbing stairs.

Gardens and Ponds:

The church is surrounded by a spacious square with landscaped gardens and reflecting pools, adding to the serene and picturesque atmosphere of the area.

Music and Events:

Karlskirche is also known for hosting concerts and musical performances. Its acoustics make it an excellent venue for experiencing classical music in an awe-inspiring setting.

Visiting Tips:

Check the official website or local tourism information for current opening hours and any special events that may be taking place.

Secession Building: Art Nouveau Showcase

The Secession Building, also known as the Wiener Secession, is an iconic Art Nouveau masterpiece located in Vienna. Designed by the architect Joseph Maria Olbrich, the building serves as a showcase for the artists of the Vienna Secession movement, a group of artists and designers who sought to break away from traditional artistic conventions and create a new, innovative aesthetic. Here's what you should know about the Secession Building:

Architecture and Design:

The Secession Building was completed in 1898 and was initially intended as an exhibition space for the Vienna Secession movement, which aimed to promote modern art and design. The exterior of the building features intricate ornamentation, including a gilded dome crowned with a laurel wreath, symbolizing victory and creativity. The motto "Der Zeit ihre Kunst. Der Kunst ihre Freiheit" (To every age its art. To every art its freedom) is displayed above the main entrance, encapsulating the movement's philosophy.

Exhibition Hall:

The main exhibition hall of the Secession Building features a distinct Art Nouveau design, characterized by curved lines, decorative details, and innovative use of materials. The Beethoven Frieze, a large mural by the famous Austrian artist Gustav Klimt, adorns one of the walls. It was created for the 14th Secession exhibition and depicts a narrative inspired by Beethoven's Ninth Symphony.

Secession Movement:

The Vienna Secession movement aimed to break away from the academic constraints of the time and embrace new forms of artistic expression. The artists sought to create a unique Austrian modern art style that would reflect the changing times.

Current Use:

The Secession Building continues to serve as an exhibition space for contemporary art. It hosts exhibitions by various artists and is a hub for those interested in exploring innovative and experimental art forms.

Ver Sacrum:

The Secession movement published its own art journal called "Ver Sacrum" (Sacred Spring), which featured articles, illustrations, and design ideas from its members. The journal contributed to the movement's influence on the European art scene.

Visiting Tips:

Check the official website for information about current exhibitions, opening hours, and any guided tours that may be available. The Secession Building is located in the vicinity of other cultural landmarks and attractions, making it a convenient stop for art enthusiasts.

ROYAL GARDENS AND PARKS

Vienna is known for its beautifully landscaped gardens and parks, many of which have a royal or imperial heritage. These green spaces offer a serene escape from the city's bustling streets and provide opportunities for leisurely strolls, picnics, and cultural experiences. Here are some of Vienna's notable royal gardens and parks:

Schönbrunn Palace Gardens

The Schönbrunn Palace Gardens, situated within the Schönbrunn Palace complex, are a splendid example of the art of landscape design and gardening. These meticulously crafted gardens complement the grandeur of the palace and provide visitors with a picturesque setting for leisure, relaxation, and exploration. Here's what you should know about the Schönbrunn Palace Gardens:

Historical Significance:

The Schönbrunn Palace Gardens have a history that dates back to the 18th century when they were designed to enhance the majestic Schönbrunn Palace. The gardens were initially inspired by French formal gardens but evolved over time to incorporate various styles, including English landscaping and Baroque elements.

Layout and Features:

The gardens cover an expansive area and are divided into different sections, each with its own character and charm. The Great Parterre, located in front of the palace, features symmetrical flowerbeds, statues, fountains, and meticulously manicured lawns. The Neptune Fountain and the Roman Ruin, both situated within the gardens, add an air of antiquity and mythology to the landscape.

Privy Garden:

The Privy Garden, located on the west side of the palace, offers a more intimate and serene atmosphere. This part of the garden features well-kept flowerbeds, ornamental plants, and architectural elements that provide a peaceful retreat for visitors.

Gloriette:

The Gloriette is a majestic structure located on a hill at the far end of the gardens. It offers panoramic views of the palace, gardens, and the city of Vienna. The Gloriette's design echoes the Neoclassical style and adds an element of architectural grandeur to the landscape.

Zoo and Maze:

The Schönbrunn Zoo, one of the oldest zoos in the world, is also located within the palace grounds. It offers visitors a chance to explore a diverse collection of animals in a well-maintained environment. The Labyrinth, a hedge maze, is a fun and interactive feature for both children and adults.

Visiting Tips:

The Schönbrunn Palace Gardens are open to the public year-round and offer different experiences throughout the seasons, from lush greenery in the summer to vibrant colors in the fall. The Gloriette can be reached via a pleasant walk uphill and rewards visitors with breathtaking views. Guided tours of the gardens and palace are available, providing insights into the historical and cultural significance of the site.

Cultural and Natural Heritage:

The Schönbrunn Palace Gardens encapsulate the fusion of art, nature, and history that defines Vienna's royal heritage. Whether you're interested in strolling among carefully tended flowerbeds, enjoying panoramic vistas, or exploring architectural marvels, the gardens offer a glimpse into the opulent lifestyle of the Habsburg monarchy while providing a tranquil respite within the bustling city.

Belvedere Gardens

The Belvedere Gardens, surrounding the Belvedere Palace complex, are a stunning testament to Baroque landscape architecture. With their intricate design, ornate fountains, grand sculptures, and meticulously maintained greenery, the gardens provide a majestic backdrop to the palaces and offer visitors a visual feast for the senses. Here's a closer look at the enchanting Belvedere Gardens:

Historical Background:

The Belvedere Palace complex consists of two palaces: the Upper Belvedere and the Lower Belvedere, connected by beautifully designed gardens. The gardens were originally designed by Johann Lucas von Hildebrandt in the 18th century as an extension of the palaces.

Upper Belvedere Garden:

The Upper Belvedere Garden features a terraced layout with wide staircases, elegant balustrades, and meticulously manicured lawns.

Fountains, statues, and sculptures are strategically placed throughout the garden, adding to the visual splendor.

Lower Belvedere Garden:

The Lower Belvedere Garden is characterized by its formal Baroque design, featuring geometric patterns, hedges, and flowerbeds. The centerpiece of the Lower Belvedere Garden is the Neptune Fountain, an intricate water feature that adds to the grandeur of the surroundings.

Orangery Garden:

The Orangery Garden is a delightful addition to the Belvedere complex. It includes a collection of citrus trees and exotic plants in a glasshouse setting. This garden offers a serene atmosphere and a wonderful place to take a leisurely stroll.

Palace Viewpoints:

The Belvedere Gardens provide various viewpoints where visitors can enjoy captivating vistas of the palaces, cascading terraces, and surrounding landscape.

Cultural Events:

The Belvedere Gardens host various cultural events, exhibitions, and seasonal displays that enhance the beauty of the space. The gardens provide an exquisite setting for outdoor concerts, artistic performances, and special occasions.

Visiting Tips:

The gardens are open year-round, and different seasons offer varying displays of color and beauty. Spring and summer are particularly vibrant times to visit. The Upper Belvedere offers an elevated view of the city, making it a popular spot for photographers. Combine your visit to the gardens with exploring the impressive art collections housed within the Upper and Lower Belvedere palaces.

Artistic Harmony:

The Belvedere Gardens beautifully exemplify the artistic harmony between nature and human design that is characteristic of the Baroque era. The symmetry, attention to detail, and opulent surroundings make the gardens a captivating place to explore, relax, and experience the grandeur of Vienna's historical heritage.

Hofburg Palace Gardens

The Hofburg Palace Gardens, nestled within the Hofburg Imperial Palace complex, offer a serene escape from the bustling city streets of Vienna. These gardens provide a tranquil oasis where visitors can enjoy lush greenery, elegant sculptures, and a peaceful ambiance, all while being surrounded by the historic grandeur of the palace. Here's a closer look at the enchanting Hofburg Palace Gardens:

Volksgarten:

The Volksgarten, or People's Garden, is a public park located adjacent to the Hofburg Palace. It's a popular spot for both locals and visitors to unwind and enjoy the outdoors. The garden is known for its splendid rose beds, which burst into vibrant colors during the blooming season. It's a romantic and picturesque setting.

Palm House:

The Palmenhaus, or Palm House, is an elegant glasshouse located within the Burggarten. It houses a diverse collection of tropical and subtropical plants, making it a peaceful haven within the city.

Burggarten:

The Burggarten, or Castle Garden, is another section of the Hofburg Palace Gardens that is open to the public. One of the notable features of the Burggarten is the statue of Wolfgang Amadeus Mozart. This statue pays homage to the famous composer who had close ties to Vienna.

Monuments and Architecture:

The gardens are adorned with sculptures, fountains, and architectural elements that reflect Vienna's rich history and cultural heritage. The statues and monuments offer insights into Vienna's artistic legacy, with references to historical figures, classical mythology, and more.

Historical Significance:

The Hofburg Palace, which overlooks these gardens, was the primary residence of the Habsburg dynasty for centuries. The gardens were often used by the imperial family for leisure and relaxation.

Tranquil Atmosphere:

The Hofburg Palace Gardens provide a calm and peaceful environment, inviting visitors to take leisurely walks, enjoy a book on a park bench, or simply soak in the beauty of the surroundings.

Visiting Tips:

The gardens are open year-round, providing different seasonal experiences. Spring and summer are ideal times to enjoy the lush greenery and blooming flowers. Combine your visit to the gardens with exploring the Hofburg Palace and its various attractions, including museums and historic sites.

Cultural and Natural Harmony:

The Hofburg Palace Gardens strike a balance between Vienna's imperial history and the tranquility of nature. Whether you're interested in strolling through flower beds, admiring sculptures, or seeking a peaceful moment amidst the city, these gardens offer a harmonious blend of culture and nature in the heart of Vienna.

Augarten

Augarten is a historic park located in Vienna that offers a peaceful escape from the city's hustle and bustle. Nestled within this green oasis is the Augarten Palace, which serves as a cultural and architectural focal point. The park's serene atmosphere, lush landscapes, and recreational opportunities make it a favorite spot for both locals and visitors. Here's a closer look at the enchanting Augarten:

Historical Significance:

The Augarten Palace, dating back to the late 17th century, is a prime example of Baroque architecture and has a rich history tied to Austrian nobility. The palace complex is known for housing the Augarten Porcelain Manufactory, which has produced exquisite porcelain for centuries.

Green Spaces and Landscapes:

The park itself offers spacious lawns, shaded pathways, and beautifully landscaped gardens where visitors can relax, have picnics, or engage in leisurely activities. Mature trees and serene ponds contribute to the park's tranquil ambiance, making it a perfect spot for unwinding and enjoying nature.

Porcelain Museum:

The Augarten Porcelain Museum, located within the palace, showcases the history of Viennese porcelain production and displays a wide array of porcelain pieces.

Children's Playground:

Augarten features a children's playground where young visitors can enjoy swings, slides, and other play equipment, making it a family-friendly destination.

Concerts and Performances:

The Augarten hosts open-air concerts and cultural events, especially during the summer months. These events offer an opportunity to enjoy music and performances in a serene setting.

Vienna Boys' Choir:

The Augarten is also home to the Vienna Boys' Choir, one of the oldest and most renowned boys' choirs in the world. The choir practices and performs at the Augarten Palace.

Viennese Coffeehouse:

The Augarten features its own coffeehouse, where visitors can indulge in traditional Viennese coffee and pastries in a charming atmosphere.

Visiting Tips:

The park is open to the public and provides a quiet retreat for relaxation and exploration. The Vienna Boys' Choir often performs at the palace, so you might have the chance to experience their beautiful music during your visit. Check the park's schedule for special events, concerts, and exhibitions that may be taking place.

Cultural and Natural Blend:

Augarten combines the elegance of historic architecture with the tranquility of nature, offering a balanced blend of cultural experiences and outdoor enjoyment. Whether you're interested in history, music, porcelain, or simply unwinding in a serene environment, Augarten offers a delightful escape from the urban surroundings of Vienna.

Lainzer Tiergarten

The Lainzer Tiergarten is a vast nature reserve and wildlife sanctuary located on the outskirts of Vienna. This pristine area provides a natural haven where visitors can escape the urban environment and immerse themselves in unspoiled landscapes, diverse wildlife, and outdoor activities. Here's a closer look at what the Lainzer Tiergarten has to offer:

Historical Background:

The Lainzer Tiergarten has a history dating back to the 16th century when it was initially established as a hunting ground for the Habsburgs. Today, the area remains a protected nature reserve, allowing visitors to experience the natural beauty of Vienna's surroundings.

Scenic Landscapes:

The Lainzer Tiergarten features a variety of landscapes, including dense forests, open meadows, rolling hills, and tranquil ponds. The diverse terrain provides a habitat for various plant and animal species, offering a glimpse of Vienna's natural biodiversity.

Hiking Trails:

The reserve is crisscrossed with well-maintained hiking trails that cater to various levels of fitness and interests. Hikers can choose from easy walks to more challenging trails, allowing them to explore the reserve at their own pace.

Wildlife Viewing:

The Lainzer Tiergarten is home to a wide range of wildlife, including deer, boars, foxes, and various bird species. Nature enthusiasts and wildlife photographers will find plenty of opportunities to observe and capture the animals in their natural habitats.

Hermesvilla:

Within the Lainzer Tiergarten, you'll find the Hermesvilla, an elegant villa that was a gift from Emperor Franz Joseph to his wife, Empress Elisabeth (Sisi). The villa is now a museum that provides insights into the life and history of the imperial couple.

Outdoor Recreation:

The Lainzer Tiergarten is a popular destination for outdoor activities such as hiking, jogging, cycling, and picnicking. It's an ideal place for those seeking fresh air, physical activity, and a connection with nature.

Visiting Tips:

The Lainzer Tiergarten is open year-round, but it's advisable to check the opening hours and trail conditions before your visit. Wear comfortable hiking shoes and bring water and snacks, especially if you plan to explore the trails. Respect the reserve's rules and regulations to ensure the protection of the wildlife and environment.

Nature's Retreat:

The Lainzer Tiergarten offers a unique opportunity to experience the natural side of Vienna and connect with the outdoors. Whether you're looking for a leisurely stroll, a challenging hike, or a chance to spot local wildlife, this nature reserve provides a serene escape where you can recharge amid Vienna's unspoiled landscapes.

Stadtpark

Stadtpark, or the City Park, is a charming green space located in the heart of Vienna. Known for its peaceful ambiance, picturesque landscapes, and artistic elements, Stadtpark offers a delightful escape for both locals and visitors. This iconic park is famous for its iconic golden statue of Johann

Strauss II and its tranquil atmosphere. Here's what you can expect to experience at Stadtpark:

Johann Strauss Monument:

The most recognizable feature of Stadtpark is the gilded statue of the "Waltz King," Johann Strauss II. This iconic statue pays tribute to the renowned composer and his contributions to Vienna's musical heritage.

Lush Landscapes:

Stadtpark is beautifully landscaped, with winding pathways, serene ponds, and well-tended lawns that provide an inviting space for relaxation and leisure.

Floral Displays:

The park features various flowerbeds that bloom with vibrant colors throughout the seasons. In the spring and summer, the park is adorned with a variety of flowers that create a visually pleasing atmosphere.

Artistic Elements:

In addition to the Strauss monument, Stadtpark boasts a collection of sculptures and statues, offering visitors an artistic experience amidst nature. The park's sculptures range from classical figures to more contemporary works, contributing to the park's unique charm.

Bridges and Water Features:

Bridges traverse the small streams and ponds within the park, providing picturesque spots for relaxation and photo opportunities. The gentle sounds of flowing water and the reflections on the ponds add to the park's serene ambiance.

Music Pavilion:

Stadtpark features a small music pavilion where occasional outdoor concerts and performances take place, creating a delightful backdrop for cultural experiences.

Local Gathering Place:

Stadtpark is a popular spot for both locals and tourists, offering a peaceful environment for picnics, reading, or simply enjoying the scenery.

Visiting Tips:

Stadtpark is open to the public and is accessible throughout the year.

Plan a leisurely stroll through the park to fully appreciate its beauty and the various sculptures and monuments. Visit the park during different times of the day to experience its changing moods and lighting.

Harmony of Art and Nature:

Stadtpark's harmonious blend of art, nature, and music captures the essence of Vienna's cultural identity. Whether you're interested in admiring sculptures, taking a peaceful walk, or simply enjoying the lush landscapes, Stadtpark offers a tranquil haven where you can immerse yourself in Vienna's artistic and natural beauty.

Schoenbrunn Palace Park

The Schönbrunn Palace Park, surrounding the iconic Schönbrunn Palace, is a masterpiece of garden design that transports visitors into a world of grandeur, elegance, and natural beauty. This meticulously landscaped park offers a harmonious blend of ornamental gardens, historical architecture, and lush greenery. Here's a closer look at the enchanting Schönbrunn Palace Park:

Historical Significance:

The Schönbrunn Palace Park has its origins in the 18th century and was designed to complement the opulence of Schönbrunn Palace itself.

It was originally conceived as a setting for various leisure activities, events, and gatherings of the Habsburg monarchy.

Great Parterre:

The Great Parterre, located in front of the palace, features symmetrical flowerbeds, neatly trimmed hedges, and grand statues that contribute to the park's elegance. It provides a sense of order and beauty that befits the grandeur of the palace.

Privy Garden:

The Privy Garden, on the west side of the palace, offers a more intimate and tranquil space. It features well-maintained flowerbeds and ornamental plants. This part of the garden is ideal for quiet contemplation and leisurely walks.

Roman Ruin and Neptune Fountain:

The Roman Ruin, an architectural folly designed to mimic ancient ruins, adds a touch of antiquity and artistry to the park. The Neptune Fountain, a magnificent water feature, brings a sense of classical mythology to the landscape.

Gloriette and Hillside Gardens:

The Gloriette, an elevated structure at the far end of the park, provides panoramic views of the palace and gardens, rewarding visitors with breathtaking vistas. The hillside gardens surrounding the Gloriette offer a serene environment for relaxation and contemplation.

Tiergarten Schönbrunn:

The Schönbrunn Zoo, also known as Tiergarten Schönbrunn, is one of the oldest zoos in the world and is located within the palace grounds.

The zoo showcases a diverse collection of animals and offers an educational and family-friendly experience.

Cultural Events:

The Schönbrunn Palace Park hosts a range of cultural events, concerts, and performances throughout the year, allowing visitors to immerse themselves in Vienna's rich artistic heritage.

Visiting Tips:

The park is open year-round, and the changing seasons bring different colors and atmospheres to the gardens. Wear comfortable shoes for exploring the expansive grounds and consider taking a guided tour to learn about the park's history and features.

Imperial Elegance and Natural Harmony:

The Schönbrunn Palace Park is a testament to the aesthetic sensibilities of the Habsburgs and their dedication to creating a harmonious blend of architecture and nature. Whether you're interested in history, horticulture, or simply enjoying the beauty of a well-designed landscape, the Schönbrunn Palace Park offers a serene and captivating experience that captures the essence of Vienna's imperial past.

Prater Park

The Prater Park, often referred to simply as "Prater," is a popular public park in Vienna known for its diverse attractions, green spaces, and recreational opportunities. This vast park is a beloved destination for both locals and tourists, offering a blend of natural beauty and entertainment options. Here's an overview of what you can experience at Prater Park:

Iconic Wiener Riesenrad:

The Wiener Riesenrad, or Vienna Giant Ferris Wheel, is one of Prater's most recognizable landmarks. It has been a symbol of Vienna since its construction in 1897 and offers panoramic views of the city.

Amusement Park:

Prater is home to an amusement park section known as the Wurstelprater, featuring a variety of rides, attractions, and games. From classic carousels to modern thrill rides, the amusement park caters to visitors of all ages, making it a family-friendly destination.

Green Spaces and Picnic Areas:

Prater Park offers vast open spaces, grassy lawns, and shaded groves, providing ample opportunities for picnics, relaxation, and outdoor activities. Locals and tourists alike enjoy leisurely walks, jogging, and bike rides within the park's expansive grounds.

Liliputbahn Miniature Railway:

The Liliputbahn is a miniature railway that takes visitors on a charming ride through Prater Park, providing a unique perspective of the surroundings.

Planetarium and Museum:

The Prater also features the Urania Observatory and Planetarium, where visitors can explore the cosmos through educational exhibits and multimedia presentations.

Gastronomic Delights:

Prater offers a variety of dining options, from traditional Viennese food stalls to international cuisine and fast food outlets. Be sure to try some classic Austrian snacks and treats while exploring the park.

Events and Festivals:

Throughout the year, Prater hosts various events, festivals, and seasonal celebrations that enhance the park's vibrant atmosphere. From concerts to cultural festivals, there's always something happening at Prater.

Visiting Tips:

Prater Park is easily accessible from the city center and is open year-round. The amusement park section has specific operating hours.

The Wiener Riesenrad offers particularly stunning views during the evening when the city lights up. While the amusement park area has entrance fees for individual rides, entry to the broader Prater Park is free.

Vibrant Recreation Hub:

Prater Park combines leisure, entertainment, and natural beauty in a dynamic urban setting. Whether you're seeking excitement on amusement rides, leisurely walks, or simply a place to relax and enjoy the outdoors, Prater offers a diverse range of experiences that capture Vienna's joyful spirit and appeal to visitors of all ages.

Volksgarten

Volksgarten, or the People's Garden, is a picturesque public park located in the heart of Vienna. This historic green space offers a serene retreat for locals and visitors alike, featuring beautifully landscaped gardens, fragrant rose beds, and charming sculptures. Here's a closer look at the enchanting Volksgarten:

Historical Background:

Volksgarten was originally created in the 19th century on the site of the old city fortifications that were dismantled. The park was designed to provide a recreational space for the citizens of Vienna and has since become a beloved destination.

Rose Garden:

One of the park's main attractions is its stunning rose garden, which features a diverse collection of rose varieties in full bloom during the spring and summer months. The well-maintained flowerbeds create a colorful and fragrant atmosphere, making it a favorite spot for both nature enthusiasts and romantics.

Classical Architecture:

Volksgarten features classical architecture that complements its greenery. The Theseus Temple, designed in the style of a Greek temple, stands as a centerpiece within the park. The temple houses a statue of the mythical Greek hero Theseus battling the Minotaur.

Sculptures and Monuments:

Throughout the park, you'll find various sculptures and monuments that celebrate figures from Vienna's history and cultural heritage. These artistic elements contribute to the park's aesthetic and provide opportunities for contemplation and admiration.

Palm House and Café:

The park features a Palm House where visitors can find tropical and subtropical plants, creating a small botanical oasis within the green surroundings. The Palm House also houses a café where you can enjoy refreshments while surrounded by lush vegetation.

Peaceful Ambiance:

Volksgarten's layout, with its well-planned paths, shaded areas, and benches, creates a peaceful atmosphere that invites visitors to unwind and relax. It's a popular spot for locals to enjoy outdoor picnics, leisurely walks, and moments of reflection.

Visiting Tips:

Volksgarten is open year-round, but the best time to appreciate the vibrant rose garden is during the spring and summer. Consider visiting during different times of the day to experience the changing lighting and ambiance. Don't forget your camera to capture the park's natural beauty and intricate details.

Natural Haven in the City:

Volksgarten is a testament to the importance of green spaces in urban environments. It offers a tranquil oasis where visitors can escape the city's hustle and bustle, immerse themselves in the beauty of nature, and enjoy the artistry of both gardens and sculptures. Whether you're seeking a peaceful stroll, a romantic setting, or a place to appreciate Vienna's cultural heritage, Volksgarten is a must-visit destination.

MUSIC AND CULTURE

Welcome to the Vienna Travel Guide for 2023 and beyond, focusing on music and culture! Vienna is renowned for its rich history, classical music heritage, stunning architecture, and vibrant cultural scene. Here's what you need to know to make the most of your visit:

Music Heritage

Vienna's music heritage is a defining feature of the city's cultural identity. As the birthplace of numerous renowned composers and a hub for musical innovation, Vienna offers a plethora of experiences for music enthusiasts:

Vienna State Opera:

The Vienna State Opera (Wiener Staatsoper) is a world-famous institution where you can witness captivating opera and ballet performances. The grand architecture and impeccable acoustics make it a must-visit for those seeking a quintessential Viennese cultural experience.

Vienna Philharmonic Orchestra:

Known for its exceptional quality and distinct sound, the Vienna Philharmonic Orchestra often performs at the Musikverein. Attending a concert here allows you to revel in the classical compositions in a venue celebrated for its stunning architecture and acoustic perfection.

House of Music (Haus der Musik):

A modern interactive museum dedicated to the world of sound and music. This immersive experience takes visitors on a journey through Vienna's musical history, showcasing the lives of great composers, allowing you to conduct virtual orchestras, and offering insights into the science of sound.

Vienna Boys' Choir (Wiener Sängerknaben):

With a history dating back over 500 years, the Vienna Boys' Choir is a living symbol of the city's musical heritage. Catch one of their performances, often held in historic churches, for a truly unique auditory experience.

Beethoven Pasqualatihaus:

Explore the former residence of Ludwig van Beethoven, located in the heart of Vienna. The Beethoven Pasqualatihaus offers a glimpse into the life of the famous composer and his creative process.

Haydnhaus:

Visit the home of Joseph Haydn, another prominent composer from the classical era. This museum provides insights into Haydn's life and works, giving you a deeper understanding of the era's music.

Viennese Waltz and Strauss:

Vienna's contribution to the world of music extends beyond classical compositions. The city is synonymous with the waltz, and the works of Johann Strauss II, known as the "Waltz King," are celebrated with performances and events.

Musical Performances Across the City:

In addition to formal concert halls, you can often find street musicians and small ensembles performing in various squares and parks. This adds to the city's overall musical atmosphere and offers opportunities for spontaneous enjoyment.

Musical Festivals:

Throughout the year, Vienna hosts various music festivals that cater to different genres, from classical to contemporary. These festivals attract international and local talent, ensuring a diverse and enriching musical experience.

Local Music Venues:

Explore local cafes, taverns, and bars where live music performances are often held. These venues showcase Vienna's dynamic music scene and might introduce you to emerging artists and unique genres.

Theater And Performances

Here's a detailed look at Vienna's theater and performance scene:

Theater and Performances:

Vienna's theatrical and performance arts scene is as diverse as it is vibrant, encompassing everything from classic theater productions to cutting-edge performances. Immerse yourself in the city's cultural richness through these experiences:

Burgtheater:

Austria's national theater, the Burgtheater, boasts a rich history of producing high-quality performances, including classical plays, contemporary dramas, and thought-provoking works. Its grand architecture and reputation for excellence make it a cornerstone of Vienna's theater scene.

Volkstheater:

Known for its commitment to socially relevant and experimental works, the Volkstheater offers an alternative perspective on theater. Its productions often address contemporary issues and challenge traditional norms.

Theater an der Wien:

This venue is dedicated to opera, operettas, and musical theater. Experience a mix of classic and modern interpretations of well-loved operatic works.

Josefstadt Theater:

The oldest still-active theater in Vienna, the Josefstadt Theater specializes in comedies, often with a Viennese twist. Its intimate setting provides a unique theatrical experience.

Leopoldstadt Theater:

Focusing on Jewish-themed performances and stories, this theater contributes to Vienna's multicultural landscape by exploring historical and contemporary narratives.

Experimental and Contemporary Theater:

Vienna's avant-garde scene thrives in smaller theaters and alternative spaces. These venues showcase experimental plays, interactive performances, and innovative storytelling methods.

Puppet Theater (Marionettentheater):

For a whimsical experience, attend a puppet theater performance. Classic operas and fairy tales are brought to life through intricately crafted puppets and impressive puppetry techniques.

Vienna International Dance Festival:

If you're a dance enthusiast, this festival features a diverse range of dance styles and performances, including contemporary, ballet, and traditional dance forms.

Vienna's Coffeehouse Culture:

Many of Vienna's historic coffeehouses host live readings, musical performances, and spoken word events. These cozy settings offer a unique blend of culture and relaxation.

Cultural and Arts Centers:

Places like the MuseumsQuartier (MQ) host interdisciplinary performances that combine theater, dance, visual arts, and more. These events provide an immersive experience that reflects the city's dynamic cultural fusion.

Street Performances:

As you stroll through Vienna's streets and squares, you might encounter street performers showcasing their talents, whether it's music, magic, or other entertaining acts.

Festival and Event Performances:

Throughout the year, Vienna hosts a variety of cultural festivals that feature theatrical performances, such as the Vienna Festival Weeks, which bring together a range of artistic disciplines.

Vienna State Opera

The Vienna State Opera (Wiener Staatsoper) is one of the most prestigious opera houses in the world, renowned for its exceptional performances, historical significance, and stunning architecture. Here's a detailed overview of this iconic institution:

History and Architecture:

The Vienna State Opera was officially opened in 1869 as the Imperial and Royal Court Opera House (Kaiserlich-königliche Hofoper) during the reign of Emperor Franz Joseph I. The architecture blends neoclassical and Renaissance elements, creating an impressive facade that reflects Vienna's rich artistic heritage.

Acoustic Excellence:

The opera house is celebrated not only for its visual splendor but also for its exceptional acoustics. Renowned conductors, musicians, and singers have praised the opera house's acoustics, which contribute to the immersive experience for both performers and audiences.

Repertoire:

The Vienna State Opera boasts an extensive repertoire that spans from traditional operas by Mozart, Beethoven, and Verdi to contemporary works by modern composers. Opera lovers can enjoy a diverse range of productions, including timeless classics, lesser-known gems, and innovative interpretations.

Operatic Performances:

The opera house hosts regular opera and ballet performances, often featuring internationally acclaimed artists. Whether you're a seasoned opera enthusiast or a newcomer to the art form, the Vienna State Opera offers a range of productions to suit various tastes.

Ballet Performances:

In addition to opera, the Vienna State Opera is also home to the Vienna State Ballet (Wiener Staatsballett). The ballet company presents a variety of classical and contemporary ballets, showcasing the artistry and technical prowess of its talented dancers.

Ticket Information:

Tickets to performances at the Vienna State Opera are highly sought after, and it's recommended to book in advance, especially for popular productions. Tickets can be purchased online through the official website or at the opera house's box office.

Standing Room Tickets:

For those looking to experience the opera on a budget, standing room tickets (Stehplatzkarten) are available for purchase on the day of the performance. These tickets provide access to designated standing areas within the opera house, allowing you to enjoy world-class performances at a lower cost.

Dress Code:

While there isn't a strict dress code, many patrons choose to dress elegantly when attending performances at the Vienna State Opera. It's common to see people in formal attire, but you'll also find a range of styles among the audience.

Tours:

If you're interested in the opera house's history, architecture, and behind-the-scenes workings, guided tours are available. These tours offer insights into the backstage areas, costume department, and the magnificent auditorium.

Season and Schedule:

The Vienna State Opera's performance schedule typically runs from September to June, with a summer break. The annual program includes a diverse selection of operas, ballets, and special events.

Haus der Musik (House of Music)

Haus der Musik, located in Vienna, is an interactive museum that celebrates the world of sound and music. This innovative museum provides visitors with a unique and engaging experience that explores the history, science, and artistic aspects of music. Here's what you can expect from your visit:

The Sound Museum:

This section delves into the science of sound and music. Visitors can experiment with various interactive displays to learn about sound waves, frequencies, and how musical instruments produce sound.

The Great Composers:

Explore the lives and works of some of the greatest composers in history, including Wolfgang Amadeus Mozart, Ludwig van Beethoven, and Franz Schubert. Learn about their achievements and contributions to the world of music.

Virtual Conductor:

Step into the shoes of a conductor and lead a virtual orchestra. Visitors can stand in front of a large screen, mimic the gestures of a conductor, and watch as the virtual orchestra responds to their movements.

Sonotopia:

This interactive sound experience allows visitors to create their own compositions using a variety of sounds and musical elements. It's a playful way to experiment with music and unleash your creativity.

Stairplay:

As you ascend the museum's staircase, you can play musical notes by stepping on specific panels, creating melodies with each step.

The Brain Opera:

This unique interactive exhibit allows visitors to collectively compose music using gesture-based technology. It's an immersive experience where participants become part of a live "brain orchestra."

Virtual Reality Sound Installation:

Some exhibits use virtual reality to immerse visitors in auditory and visual experiences that showcase the power of music and sound.

Audio Guide:

The museum offers audio guides in multiple languages, providing detailed information about each exhibit and enhancing your overall experience.

Family-Friendly:

Haus der Musik is suitable for visitors of all ages, making it a great destination for families and individuals alike.

Plan Ahead:

The museum can get busy, especially during peak tourist seasons. Consider visiting during off-peak hours or purchasing tickets in advance to avoid long lines.

Duration:

The amount of time you spend in the museum can vary depending on your level of engagement with the exhibits. On average, visitors spend around 1.5 to 2 hours exploring.

Accessibility:

The museum is generally accessible to individuals with mobility challenges. Elevators and ramps are available to ensure that everyone can enjoy the exhibits.

Wolfgang Amadeus Mozart

Life and Work:

Mozart arrived in Vienna in 1781, seeking better opportunities for his music career. He was already well-known as a child prodigy and had composed numerous works by this time. During his time in Vienna, Mozart composed some of his most famous and enduring works, including operas like "The Marriage of Figaro" and "Don Giovanni," as well as symphonies, chamber music, and piano concertos. Despite his musical brilliance, Mozart faced financial challenges throughout his Vienna years, and he often struggled to find steady patronage.

Legacy:

Today, Mozart's presence is felt throughout Vienna. Visitors can explore places associated with him, such as his former residences and the locations where he premiered many of his works. The Mozarthaus Vienna is a museum located in the house where Mozart lived from 1784 to 1787. It offers insights into his life and the music of his era.

Ludwig van Beethoven

Life and Work:

Beethoven moved to Vienna in 1792 to study with Joseph Haydn and further his musical career. He quickly gained a reputation as a virtuoso pianist and a composer with innovative ideas. During his time in Vienna, Beethoven composed some of his most celebrated works, including his symphonies, piano sonatas, and string quartets. Notably, his Ninth Symphony premiered in Vienna in 1824. Beethoven's career was marked by personal challenges, including his struggle with deafness, which he battled while continuing to create groundbreaking music.

Legacy:

Beethoven's impact on Vienna is profound. His music bridged the gap between the classical and romantic eras, and his compositions remain central to the classical repertoire. Beethoven's apartment, known as the Pasqualatihaus, has been preserved as a museum that offers insights into his life and works during his time in Vienna.

Cultural Events

Vienna is a city that thrives on its vibrant cultural scene, offering a plethora of events and festivals throughout the year. These events showcase the city's rich history, artistic heritage, and contemporary creativity. Here are some notable cultural events in Vienna:

Vienna Festival Weeks (Wiener Festwochen):

Taking place during May and June, the Vienna Festival Weeks are a highlight of the city's cultural calendar. This multidisciplinary festival features a diverse range of performances, including theater, opera, dance, music, and visual arts. International artists and renowned ensembles participate, presenting innovative and thought-provoking works.

Vienna Opera Ball:

Held annually in February at the Vienna State Opera, the Opera Ball is a glamorous and elegant event that brings together high society, diplomats, and opera enthusiasts. The opera house transforms into a grand ballroom, and guests can enjoy waltzing to live classical music performances.

Vienna Jazz Festival:

Music lovers will appreciate the Vienna Jazz Festival, which takes place in June and July. The festival hosts world-class jazz musicians and offers performances ranging from traditional jazz to contemporary fusion.

Vienna International Film Festival (Viennale):

Film enthusiasts should not miss the Viennale, which occurs in October. This international film festival showcases a wide array of films, from art-house productions to avant-garde cinema.

Vienna Design Week:

For design aficionados, the Vienna Design Week in September provides a platform to explore contemporary design, architecture, and innovative ideas through exhibitions, workshops, and installations.

Vienna Literature Festival (Literaturfest Wien):

Literature enthusiasts can enjoy the Literaturfest Wien, a literary festival that features readings, discussions, and talks by Austrian and international authors. It usually takes place in November.

Vienna Pride:

Vienna Pride is a colorful celebration of LGBTQ+ rights and diversity that includes a vibrant parade, concerts, parties, and discussions. It occurs in June and fosters an inclusive atmosphere in the city.

Christmas Markets:

During the Advent season, Vienna's Christmas markets (Christkindlmärkte) transform the city into a winter wonderland. These markets offer traditional crafts, holiday treats, and festive decorations, creating a magical atmosphere.

Long Night of Museums (Lange Nacht der Museen):

During this event, museums, galleries, and cultural institutions open their doors late into the night, allowing visitors to explore Vienna's art and culture scene in a unique way. It's usually held in October.

Vienna Biennale for Change:

This interdisciplinary event, occurring in various venues across the city, focuses on addressing current societal challenges through art, design, and architecture. It encourages conversations about sustainability, innovation, and social change.

COFFEE CULTURE AND CUISINE

Vienna is renowned for its rich coffee culture and culinary traditions. The city's coffeehouses are not just places to enjoy a cup of coffee; they are hubs of social interaction, artistic inspiration, and historical significance. In addition to its coffee culture, Vienna offers a diverse array of traditional and modern cuisine. Here's what you need to know about experiencing coffee culture and cuisine in Vienna:

Traditional Coffeehouses

Vienna's traditional coffeehouses, known as "Kaffeehäuser," hold a special place in the city's culture and history. These establishments are more than just places to have a cup of coffee; they are hubs of social interaction, intellectual exchange, and artistic inspiration. Stepping into a Viennese coffeehouse is like stepping back in time to an era of leisurely conversations, literary discussions, and the enjoyment of coffee specialties. Here's a closer look at Vienna's traditional coffeehouses:

Historical Significance:

Vienna's coffeehouse tradition dates back to the 17th century when the city's first coffeehouse, Café Frauenhuber, opened its doors in 1685.

These coffeehouses quickly became gathering places for intellectuals, artists, writers, and philosophers. They were venues for discussions, debates, and the exchange of ideas.

Distinctive Atmosphere:

The atmosphere in Viennese coffeehouses is relaxed and unhurried. It's common to linger for hours over a single cup of coffee while reading newspapers, engaging in conversation, or people-watching. Many coffeehouses feature elegant interiors with plush seating, marble tabletops, chandeliers, and ornate decor that harkens back to the 19th and early 20th centuries.

Menu Offerings:

Viennese coffeehouses offer a variety of coffee specialties that go beyond the standard espresso and cappuccino. Some popular options include the Wiener Melange, Einspänner, and Kleiner Brauner. The coffee is often accompanied by a wide range of delectable pastries and desserts, including classics like Sachertorte, apfelstrudel, and linzer torte.

Culinary and Cultural Traditions:

Coffeehouses are places where people from all walks of life gather, from students to professionals to retirees. The environment fosters a sense of inclusivity and community. The newspapers provided in many coffeehouses allow patrons to catch up on current events while enjoying their coffee. Viennese coffeehouses also serve as venues for cultural events such as readings, musical performances, and artistic exhibitions.

Famous Coffeehouses:

Some of Vienna's most famous coffeehouses have historical significance. Café Central, for instance, was frequented by luminaries like Freud, Trotsky, and Zweig. Café Hawelka is known for its bohemian atmosphere and Viennese charm.

Preservation of Tradition:

The traditional coffeehouse culture in Vienna is carefully preserved to maintain its historical and cultural value. Regulations and guidelines ensure that the authentic ambiance remains intact.

Visiting Tips:

- ❖ Take your time when visiting a traditional coffeehouse. Order a coffee, indulge in a pastry, and enjoy the unhurried atmosphere.

- ❖ Remember that tipping is customary in Vienna, so it's polite to leave a small tip for the service.

Naschmarkt

The Naschmarkt is one of Vienna's most iconic and lively markets, offering a sensory-rich experience that showcases the city's diverse culinary offerings. This bustling market is a paradise for food enthusiasts, offering a wide range of fresh produce, specialty foods, international cuisine, and a vibrant atmosphere. Here's what you need to know about the Naschmarkt:

History and Origins:

The Naschmarkt has a history that dates back to the 16th century when it was primarily a trading hub for dairy products. The market's name, "Naschmarkt," originates from the German word "naschen," which means to snack or nibble.

Diverse Offerings:

The Naschmarkt is known for its extensive selection of fresh fruits, vegetables, spices, herbs, meats, cheeses, and seafood. In addition to raw ingredients, the market features numerous stalls offering prepared foods, international cuisines, street food, and gourmet delicacies.

Specialty Shops:

You'll find specialty shops offering exotic fruits, regional cheeses, olives, nuts, dried fruits, and more. The Naschmarkt is also home to shops that sell international foods and ingredients, catering to Vienna's multicultural population.

Restaurants and Street Food:

The market is lined with restaurants, cafes, and street food stalls where you can sample dishes from various cuisines, including Middle Eastern, Mediterranean, Asian, and traditional Austrian.

Culinary Events:

The Naschmarkt hosts various culinary events, food festivals, and market days that celebrate seasonal produce and international flavors.

Antiques and Flea Market:

In addition to food, the Naschmarkt features an antiques and flea market section where you can find vintage items, collectibles, and unique treasures.

Atmosphere and Vibrancy:

The market is known for its bustling energy, vibrant colors, and the lively interactions between vendors and customers. It's a great place for people-watching, exploring, and immersing yourself in Vienna's diverse culinary scene.

Visiting Tips:

- The Naschmarkt is open every day except Sundays, and it's most lively during the mornings and early afternoons.
- Wear comfortable shoes and be prepared to spend time exploring the various stalls and sampling different foods.
- Bring cash, as some vendors might not accept credit cards.

Coffee Specialties

Vienna is famous for its rich coffee culture, and it offers a variety of unique coffee specialties that reflect the city's history, ambiance, and love for all things coffee. Here are some of the most iconic Viennese coffee specialties that you must try during your visit:

Wiener Melange:

Similar to a cappuccino, the Wiener Melange is a combination of espresso and steamed milk, often topped with a dollop of milk foam. It strikes a perfect balance between the richness of espresso and the creaminess of milk.

Einspänner:

This strong black coffee is served in a glass topped with a generous dollop of whipped cream. The contrast between the bitter coffee and the sweet cream is a delight to the taste buds.

Verlängerter:

Translating to "extended" or "lengthened," the Verlängerter is similar to an Americano. It's made by adding hot water to an espresso, creating a milder and larger coffee drink.

Kleiner Brauner:

A "small brown" coffee, the Kleiner Brauner is a shot of espresso served with a small amount of milk or cream on the side. It's a simple yet satisfying option for those who prefer their coffee on the stronger side.

Mélange:

This coffee specialty is a mix of coffee and milk, similar to a latte. It's often served with a little milk foam on top and is a popular choice for those who enjoy a creamy coffee.

Maria Theresia:

Named after the Austrian empress Maria Theresa, this coffee drink combines equal parts of coffee and hot chocolate. It's a sweet and indulgent option for those with a sweet tooth.

Pharisäer:

A decadent coffee cocktail, the Pharisäer combines coffee, rum, whipped cream, and sugar. It's a warming and spirited drink often enjoyed during colder months.

Eiskaffee:

Perfect for the warmer months, the Eiskaffee is a chilled coffee drink made with coffee, ice cream, and whipped cream. It's a delightful treat to cool off while still enjoying your coffee fix.

Kaisermelange:

A coffee with a royal touch, the Kaisermelange is a mix of coffee, egg yolk, honey, and cognac, resulting in a rich and flavorful beverage.

Franziskaner:

A "Franciscan" coffee, the Franziskaner is a mélange with whipped cream instead of milk foam. It's a creamy and satisfying option for those who prefer a richer coffee experience.

Viennese Sachertorte

Sachertorte is a world-famous Viennese dessert that holds a special place in Austria's culinary heritage. This decadent chocolate cake is beloved for its rich flavor, smooth texture, and the layer of apricot jam that adds a unique twist to its taste. Here's everything you need to know about this iconic Viennese treat:

History and Origin:

Sachertorte was created in 1832 by Franz Sacher, a young apprentice chef at the court of Prince Klemens Wenzel von Metternich in Vienna.

The dessert was originally made for an important event when the head chef was unexpectedly absent. Franz Sacher's creation became an instant hit.

Ingredients and Preparation:

Sachertorte is a dense and moist chocolate cake with layers of apricot jam and a smooth chocolate glaze. The cake is made using high-quality dark chocolate and cocoa, which contribute to its rich chocolatey flavor. The layer of apricot jam adds a layer of fruitiness that balances the sweetness of the cake and complements the chocolate.

Serving and Accompaniments:

Sachertorte is traditionally served with a dollop of whipped cream on the side. The cream helps balance the richness of the cake. It's often enjoyed with a cup of coffee or tea, making it a quintessential part of Vienna's coffeehouse culture.

Sachertorte at Hotel Sacher:

The original recipe for Sachertorte is a well-guarded secret, passed down through generations of the Sacher family. The Hotel Sacher, founded by Franz Sacher's son, Eduard Sacher, is renowned for serving the most famous version of

Sachertorte. The hotel's Café Sacher is a destination for both locals and visitors seeking an authentic Sachertorte experience.

Tradition and Celebration:

Sachertorte has become a symbol of Austrian cuisine and is often associated with celebrations and special occasions. It's also a popular souvenir for tourists visiting Vienna, with many purchasing boxed Sachertorte as gifts to take back home.

Viennese Culinary Heritage:

Sachertorte is not only a delicious dessert but also a reflection of Vienna's rich culinary heritage and the importance of sweets in Austrian culture.

Visiting Tips:

- ❖ If you're in Vienna, consider visiting Café Sacher at the Hotel Sacher to enjoy an authentic Sachertorte experience in a historic setting.

- ❖ You can also find Sachertorte in various cafes, restaurants, and bakeries throughout Vienna.

ACTIVITIES

Here are some activities you can consider during your visit to Vienna:

Strolls and Hikes

Vienna offers a variety of strolls and hikes that allow you to enjoy the city's natural beauty, parks, and scenic landscapes. Here are some options for leisurely strolls and more active hikes:

Stadtpark Stroll:

Take a leisurely walk through Stadtpark, known for its lush greenery, sculptures, and the famous golden statue of Johann Strauss II.

Prater Park Walk:

Explore the extensive Prater Park, featuring wide paths, open spaces, and the iconic Giant Ferris Wheel.

Belvedere Gardens Stroll:

Wander through the beautifully landscaped gardens of Belvedere Palace, featuring fountains, sculptures, and stunning flower beds.

Schönbrunn Palace Gardens:

Enjoy a stroll in the vast gardens of Schönbrunn Palace, filled with well-maintained paths, ornamental structures, and a zoo.

Lainzer Tiergarten Hike:

Venture into the Lainzer Tiergarten, a nature reserve within the city, for hiking trails, dense forests, and wildlife.

Vienna Woods (Wienerwald) Hikes:

Explore the Vienna Woods with various hiking trails catering to different levels of fitness. Paths range from easy to more challenging.

Danube Island (Donauinsel) Walk:

Walk along the scenic Danube Island, a long and narrow recreational area offering paths, green spaces, and riverside views.

Kahlenberg Hike:

Hike up Kahlenberg for panoramic views of Vienna and the surrounding countryside. The peak is accessible by trails and a road.

Cobenzl and Leopoldsberg Hike:

Hike from Cobenzl to Leopoldsberg for breathtaking views of the city and the Danube River.

Vienna's Vineyards Stroll:

Take a leisurely stroll through Vienna's vineyards, such as those in Grinzing or Nussdorf, and enjoy views of the city and the Danube.

Wilhelminenberg Park and Villa Hike:

Explore the beautiful park surrounding Villa Aurora on Wilhelminenberg hill for scenic vistas and historical charm.

Donaupark Stroll:

Stroll through Donaupark, which features wide walking paths, colorful flower displays, and the iconic Danube Tower.

Türkenschanzpark Walk:

Enjoy a peaceful walk through Türkenschanzpark, known for its tranquility, historic monuments, and botanical diversity.

Schwarzenbergpark Hike:

Discover Schwarzenbergpark, offering forested paths, open meadows, and a chance to escape the urban environment.

These strolls and hikes provide a range of options for experiencing

Cruises

Vienna's location along the Danube River offers the perfect opportunity for river cruises that provide scenic views of the

city and the surrounding countryside. Here are some popular cruise options:

Danube River Sightseeing Cruises:

Enjoy a leisurely cruise along the Danube River, taking in the iconic sights of Vienna, including the Vienna State Opera, Belvedere Palace, and the Danube Tower.

Evening Dinner Cruises:

Experience the romance of Vienna by taking an evening dinner cruise on the Danube, where you can savor a delicious meal while enjoying the illuminated cityscape.

Wachau Valley River Cruises:

Embark on a longer cruise that takes you through the picturesque Wachau Valley, where you'll pass charming villages, vineyards, and medieval castles.

Danube Canal Cruises:

Explore the hidden gems of Vienna along the Danube Canal, which runs through the heart of the city. These cruises offer unique views of urban landscapes and street art.

Full-Day Danube Cruises:

Consider taking a full-day cruise that covers a broader stretch of the Danube, allowing you to explore both upstream and downstream destinations.

Themed Cruises:

Some cruise operators offer themed cruises, such as jazz or classical music cruises, providing entertainment as you enjoy the river views.

Bratislava Day Cruise:

Take a day cruise to Bratislava, Slovakia, and explore the neighboring capital city before returning to Vienna.

Vienna Woods (Wienerwald) Cruises:

Enjoy cruises that navigate through the Vienna Woods, offering scenic views of the lush landscapes surrounding the city.

Special Events and Fireworks Cruises:

During special events and fireworks displays, some operators offer cruises that provide front-row seats to the festivities.

Private and Customized Cruises:

If you're looking for a more personalized experience, you can consider booking a private cruise or customizing your cruise route.

Biking

Biking in Vienna offers a fantastic way to explore the city's attractions, parks, and scenic routes. With well-maintained bike paths and bike-friendly infrastructure, you can enjoy a leisurely ride or an active adventure through the city. Here are some biking options and routes in Vienna:

City Center Exploration:

Rent a bike and explore Vienna's historic city center. Ride around the Ringstrasse, passing by iconic landmarks like the Vienna State Opera, Hofburg Palace, and Parliament.

Prater Park Cycling:

Cycle through the spacious Prater Park, enjoying the wide paths and green spaces. Visit the iconic Giant Ferris Wheel and explore the park's attractions.

Danube Island (Donauinsel) Ride:

Bike along the scenic Danube Island, a long recreational area with dedicated bike lanes and beautiful riverside views.

Danube Canal Cycling:

Explore the bike paths along the Danube Canal, passing by unique street art, trendy cafes, and picturesque bridges.

Vienna Woods (Wienerwald) Trails:

Venture into the Vienna Woods for more challenging mountain biking trails. The hills surrounding Vienna offer a variety of routes for different skill levels.

Vineyard Routes in Grinzing and Nussdorf:

Cycle through the vineyards of Grinzing and Nussdorf, enjoying the beautiful landscapes and stopping at Heurigen (wine taverns) for refreshments.

Alte Donau (Old Danube) Ride:

Bike along the shores of the Alte Donau, a former branch of the Danube. Enjoy serene waterside views and the relaxing atmosphere.

Lainzer Tiergarten Trails:

For a mix of nature and biking, explore the trails in Lainzer Tiergarten, a nature reserve that offers a chance to spot wildlife.

Pratercottage to Kahlenberg Route:

Enjoy a scenic route that takes you from Pratercottage to Kahlenberg, offering rewarding views of Vienna and the surrounding landscape.

Vienna to Klosterneuburg Route:

Take a longer ride from Vienna to Klosterneuburg, visiting the Klosterneuburg Monastery and enjoying the riverside paths.

Horse-Drawn Carriage Rides

Experiencing Vienna through a horse-drawn carriage ride is a charming and nostalgic way to explore the city's historic streets, landmarks, and parks. These rides allow you to slow down and enjoy the scenery while feeling transported back in time. Here's what you need to know about horse-drawn carriage rides in Vienna:

Starting Points:

Horse-drawn carriage rides are available in popular tourist areas such as the Stephansplatz, Hofburg Palace, and Stadtpark. You can also find carriage stands near major attractions like Schönbrunn Palace and Prater Park.

Routes and Duration:

Carriage rides often have set routes that take you past key landmarks and attractions. Common routes include rides through the historic city center, around the Ringstrasse, or through parks like Schönbrunn Palace Gardens.

Types of Carriages:

Carriages come in various sizes and styles, from traditional fiaker carriages to more ornate and luxurious options. Some carriages are open, while others have covers for protection from weather elements.

Romantic and Scenic:

Horse-drawn carriage rides are particularly popular for couples seeking a romantic experience, especially during evening rides.

Commentary:

Some carriage drivers provide commentary about the sights and history of Vienna as you ride.

Booking and Availability:

Carriage rides can be booked on the spot at designated carriage stands or in advance through various tour operators. Availability may vary depending on the season, weather, and demand.

Combination Packages:

Some carriage ride operators offer combination packages that include a ride and tickets to nearby attractions.

Customized Rides:

Some operators allow you to customize the route or length of the ride, making it a more tailored experience.

Romantic Activities

Vienna's enchanting ambiance, historic architecture, and cultural offerings make it an ideal destination for romantic experiences. Whether you're visiting with a partner or looking to create special moments, here are some romantic activities to consider in Vienna:

Horse-Drawn Carriage Ride:

Take a leisurely horse-drawn carriage ride through Vienna's historic streets and landmarks, enjoying the charm of the city together.

Evening Concert or Opera:

Attend a classical music concert or opera performance at venues like the Vienna State Opera or Musikverein, sharing a cultural experience.

Sunset at Belvedere Palace:

Visit Belvedere Palace during sunset for a romantic stroll through its beautifully lit gardens and enjoy panoramic views of the city.

Danube River Dinner Cruise:

Indulge in a romantic dinner cruise along the Danube River, savoring delicious cuisine and the city's illuminated skyline.

Candlelit Dinner at a Heurigen:

Enjoy a candlelit dinner at a traditional Heurigen (wine tavern) in Grinzing or Nussdorf, savoring local wines and Austrian dishes.

Evening Stroll along the Danube:

Take a peaceful evening walk along the Danube River, with the city lights reflecting on the water.

Coffeehouse Date:

Spend a cozy afternoon at one of Vienna's historic coffeehouses, sharing conversations over coffee and Viennese pastries.

Schönbrunn Palace Gardens:

Enjoy a romantic walk through the gardens of Schönbrunn Palace, with its fountains, sculptures, and serene atmosphere.

Romantic Photoshoot:

Capture your moments together with a romantic photoshoot at iconic locations like St. Stephen's Cathedral or the Belvedere Palace.

Wine Tasting Tour:

Embark on a wine tasting tour of Vienna's vineyards, exploring the countryside and enjoying the flavors of Austrian wines.

Hot Air Balloon Ride:

Experience Vienna from a unique perspective by taking a hot air balloon ride, enjoying breathtaking views from above.

Private Evening Tour of Palaces:

Arrange a private evening tour of imperial palaces like Schönbrunn or Hofburg, with personalized guides to add a touch of exclusivity.

Romantic Parks and Gardens:

Spend quiet moments in romantic parks like Augarten or Volksgarten, perfect for intimate conversations and relaxation.

Vienna Woods Getaway:

Plan a day trip to the Vienna Woods, enjoying outdoor activities, picnics, and the natural beauty of the surrounding countryside.

Watch the Sunrise at Kahlenberg:

Begin your day by watching the sunrise from Kahlenberg, offering a breathtaking start to a romantic day together.

Visit Vienna's Wine Taverns

Visiting Vienna's traditional wine taverns, known as "Heurigen," is a delightful way to experience the city's local culture, enjoy Austrian wines, and savor authentic cuisine. Heurigen are charming and rustic establishments where you can relax, unwind, and immerse yourself in a unique Viennese tradition. Here's what you need to know about visiting Heurigen:

Atmosphere and Ambiance:

Heurigen exude a cozy and welcoming atmosphere, often featuring outdoor seating in garden-like settings. Decor is rustic and charming, creating a relaxed and convivial environment.

Wine Selection:

Heurigen offer a selection of wines produced by local vineyards. Try traditional Austrian varieties such as Grüner Veltliner and Gemischter Satz. Some Heurigen serve their own wines, making for an authentic tasting experience.

Buffet Style:

Many Heurigen offer a buffet-style spread known as "Brettljause." This typically includes various cold cuts, cheeses, bread, and local specialties.

Live Music:

Some Heurigen feature live music, often showcasing traditional Austrian folk music, enhancing the festive ambiance.

Opening Times:

Heurigen are typically open during specific periods known as "Heuriger seasons," which vary throughout the year. The opening times are regulated by law to ensure that only new wines are served.

Location:

Vienna has several areas known for their Heurigen culture, including Grinzing, Neustift am Walde, and Nussdorf. You can easily find signs indicating open Heurigen in these areas.

How to Choose a Heurigen:

Look for a "Buschenschank" sign, indicating that the establishment is licensed to serve its own wine and food. Ask locals or consult travel guides for recommendations on popular Heurigen.

Etiquette:

You can bring your own snacks to some Heurigen, but be sure to order their wine. Tipping is customary in Austria, so it's polite to leave a tip for the service.

Relax and Enjoy:

Heurigen are about savoring the moment, so take your time to enjoy the food, wine, and company.

Combine with a Walk:

Make your Heurigen visit part of a larger experience by combining it with a walk through the vineyards or nearby parks.

Outdoor Activities

Vienna offers a variety of outdoor activities that allow you to enjoy the city's natural beauty, green spaces, and recreational opportunities. Whether you're looking for leisurely strolls, active pursuits, or relaxation, there's something for everyone to enjoy outdoors in Vienna:

Park Exploration:

Explore the beautifully landscaped gardens of Schönbrunn Palace or enjoy a leisurely stroll through Prater Park.

Discover the historic monuments and tranquil atmosphere of Stadtpark, home to the famous Johann Strauss statue.

Biking and Cycling:

Rent a bike and explore Vienna's numerous bike paths, such as those along the Danube Canal or through the Vienna Woods. Join guided bike tours that provide insight into Vienna's history and landmarks.

Danube Island (Donauinsel):

Enjoy a bike ride, jog, or leisurely walk along the picturesque Danube Island, a popular recreational area.

Boating and Kayaking:

Rent a paddleboat or kayak to explore the serene waters of the Alte Donau (Old Danube) or take a boat cruise along the Danube River.

Picnicking:

Pack a picnic and relax in one of Vienna's parks, such as Augarten or Türkenschanzpark.

Wildlife Watching:

Visit Lainzer Tiergarten to observe wildlife in their natural habitat, including deer and wild boars.

Outdoor Swimming Pools:

Cool off in the summer by visiting Vienna's outdoor swimming pools, such as the Gänsehäufel or Schafbergbad.

Outdoor Yoga and Fitness Classes:

Join outdoor yoga classes held in parks or participate in outdoor fitness activities to stay active.

Tennis and Sports:

Play tennis at public courts in parks like Stadtpark or Donaupark, or engage in other sports like basketball and soccer.

Horseback Riding:

Experience horseback riding in Vienna's outskirts, enjoying the natural landscapes and peaceful surroundings.

Outdoor Markets and Flea Markets:

Explore outdoor markets like the Naschmarkt, offering a variety of foods, products, and local specialties.

Golfing:

Enjoy a round of golf at golf courses in Vienna and its vicinity.

Relaxation by the Water:

Find a cozy spot by the water's edge along the Alte Donau or New Danube to read, relax, or simply soak up the sun.

City Views from Hills and Lookouts:

Hike up Kahlenberg or Leopoldsberg for stunning panoramic views of Vienna and the Danube.

Skateboarding and Rollerblading:

Join the local skate scene at popular spots like the MuseumsQuartier or the Danube Island skate park.

Urban Gardening:

Discover community gardens and urban gardening initiatives that allow you to get your hands dirty and grow plants.

Water Sports

While Vienna isn't typically associated with water sports like coastal cities, it still offers some opportunities for water-based activities due to its proximity to the Danube River and various water bodies. Here are a few water sports and activities you can enjoy in and around Vienna:

Canoeing and Kayaking:

Rent a canoe or kayak to paddle along the Danube River or the Alte Donau (Old Danube), enjoying the serene waters and city views.

Stand-Up Paddleboarding (SUP):

Try stand-up paddleboarding on the calm waters of the Alte Donau or Donauinsel, providing a unique way to explore the city's waterways.

Rowing:

Some areas of the Alte Donau offer rowing opportunities, allowing you to engage in a relaxing water activity.

Sailing:

Enjoy sailing on the Alte Donau or the Neusiedler See, a large lake located near Vienna that offers sailing and windsurfing opportunities.

Swimming:

During the warmer months, you can enjoy swimming in designated areas of the Danube, Alte Donau, and other lakes in the region.

Windsurfing:

If you're an experienced windsurfer, consider heading to the Neusiedler See for windsurfing adventures.

Danube Island Beaches:

Relax on the sandy beaches of Danube Island (Donauinsel) during the summer months, offering opportunities for sunbathing and swimming.

Danube River Cruises:

While not a water sport per se, Danube River cruises provide a scenic way to enjoy the water and city views.

Waterfront Dining:

Enjoy a meal at one of the waterfront restaurants along the Danube, combining dining with a view.

Beach Volleyball:

Some areas of the Danube Island have beach volleyball courts, offering a recreational activity for groups.

Fishing:

If you're interested in fishing, check local regulations and permits for fishing in the Danube and other water bodies.

Outdoor Pools and Baths:

Visit outdoor swimming pools and baths like Gänsehäufel and Schafbergbad, where you can cool off and enjoy the water during the summer.

Kid-Friendly Activities

Vienna is a family-friendly city with a range of activities that cater to children of all ages. From interactive museums to parks and attractions, here are some kid-friendly activities to consider during your visit:

Schönbrunn Palace and Zoo:

Explore the magnificent Schönbrunn Palace and its gardens. Don't miss the Schönbrunn Zoo, one of the oldest zoos in the world, which offers a variety of animals and exhibits.

Prater Park:

Enjoy family fun at Prater Park, home to the iconic Giant Ferris Wheel and a range of attractions, including an amusement park and playgrounds.

Natural History Museum (Naturhistorisches Museum):

Visit the Natural History Museum, where kids can marvel at dinosaur skeletons, gemstones, and interactive exhibits.

Technical Museum (Technisches Museum Wien):

Explore the Technical Museum, offering interactive displays on technology, transport, and inventions.

Vienna Woods (Wienerwald):

Take a family hike or bike ride in the Vienna Woods, providing outdoor adventure and fresh air.

Haus der Musik:

Discover the interactive House of Music, where children can explore sound, music, and even conduct an orchestra.

Zoom Children's Museum:

Enjoy the Zoom Children's Museum, where hands-on exhibits encourage creativity and learning.

Danube Park (Donaupark):

Visit Donaupark for open spaces, playgrounds, and the iconic Danube Tower, offering panoramic views of the city.

Prater Museum:

Learn about the history of Prater Park and its attractions at the Prater Museum, which showcases memorabilia from the amusement park's past.

Children's Farm at Lainzer Tiergarten:

Visit the Children's Farm within Lainzer Tiergarten to interact with animals and enjoy a day in nature.

Vienna's House of the Sea (Haus des Meeres):

Discover Vienna's House of the Sea, a fascinating aquarium featuring a wide range of aquatic life.

Leopold Museum Family Sundays:

Join Leopold Museum's Family Sundays for interactive art workshops designed for children and parents.

Puppet Theatre Performances:

Attend puppet theatre performances at venues like Schubert Theater, offering entertainment for young audiences.

Ice Skating in Winter:

During the winter months, enjoy ice skating at outdoor rinks like the Wiener Eislaufverein or Rathausplatz.

Children's Bookstores and Libraries:

Visit children's bookstores and libraries like the Children's Library at the Austrian National Library for storytelling and reading activities.

Danube Island Playgrounds:

Explore the numerous playgrounds along the Danube Island, providing kids with opportunities to play and interact.

Group Activities

Vienna offers a variety of group activities that are perfect for friends, family gatherings, or team outings. Whether you're interested in cultural experiences, outdoor adventures, or social activities, there's something for every group to enjoy in the city. Here are some group-friendly activities to consider:

Group Bike Tours:

Explore Vienna's landmarks and neighborhoods on a guided group bike tour, learning about the city's history and culture while staying active.

Group Segway Tours:

Experience the city on a Segway tour, a fun and unique way to cover more ground while enjoying the sights.

Escape Room Games:

Engage in a thrilling and team-building activity by participating in an escape room game, solving puzzles and mysteries together.

Cooking Classes:

Join a cooking class as a group to learn how to prepare traditional Austrian dishes or international cuisines.

Group River Cruises:

Take a group river cruise along the Danube to enjoy scenic views of the city and its landmarks from the water.

Wine Tasting Tours:

Embark on a wine tasting tour in Vienna's vineyards, enjoying group wine tastings and learning about Austrian wines.

Group Art Classes:

Participate in group art classes, such as painting or pottery workshops, to unleash your creativity together.

Group Dance Classes:

Enjoy dance classes as a group, whether it's learning the waltz or trying out a modern dance style.

Trampoline Parks:

Have an active and energetic outing at one of Vienna's trampoline parks, perfect for groups looking for fun and exercise.

Outdoor Team Building Activities:

Participate in outdoor team building activities like scavenger hunts, orienteering, or obstacle courses in Vienna's parks.

Group Theater and Performances:

Attend a theater performance, comedy show, or musical together for an entertaining night out.

Group Karaoke Nights:

Enjoy a lively group karaoke night at one of Vienna's karaoke bars or venues.

Group Spa Day:

Relax and unwind together at a spa or wellness center, enjoying massages, saunas, and relaxation treatments.

Group Picnics in Parks:

Organize a group picnic in Vienna's parks, bringing along delicious food and enjoying the outdoors.

Group Volunteering:

Participate in group volunteering activities to give back to the community while bonding with your group.

Group Wine and Dine:

Explore Vienna's culinary scene as a group by going on a food tour, trying out local restaurants, or dining in traditional Heurigen.

DAY TRIPS AND EXCURSIONS

Vienna's central location in Europe makes it an ideal starting point for day trips and excursions to nearby attractions and charming towns. Whether you're interested in exploring historic sites, enjoying natural beauty, or immersing yourself in local culture, there are plenty of options for memorable day trips from Vienna. Here are some popular destinations to consider:

Wachau Valley

Located along the Danube River, the Wachau Valley is known for its picturesque landscapes, charming villages, and vineyards. Visit towns like Dürnstein and Melk, where you can explore medieval architecture and the stunning Melk Abbey. Enjoy a leisurely boat cruise along the Danube to take in the scenic beauty of the region.

Schönbrunn Palace and Gardens

While Schönbrunn Palace is a major attraction in Vienna, its extensive gardens and grounds are perfect for a day trip. Explore the beautifully landscaped gardens, visit the Palm House, and admire the Gloriette overlooking the palace.

Bratislava, Slovakia

Just an hour's boat ride or train journey away, Bratislava offers a taste of another Central European capital. Explore the historic Old Town, visit Bratislava Castle, and enjoy the charming cafes and shops.

Salzburg

The birthplace of Mozart and the setting for "The Sound of Music," Salzburg is a cultural gem. Explore the historic Old Town, visit the Hohensalzburg Fortress, and take in the stunning Alpine scenery.

Budapest, Hungary

While a bit farther, Budapest is reachable by train and offers a day of exploring the Danube's other beautiful capital. Highlights include Buda Castle, Fisherman's Bastion, and the thermal baths.

Lake Neusiedl

This picturesque lake, located near Vienna, is a haven for outdoor enthusiasts. Enjoy sailing, swimming, cycling, and bird-watching in the unique natural landscape.

Graz

The capital of Styria, Graz is known for its historic architecture, including the Schlossberg hill with its clock tower. Explore the charming Old Town, designated as a UNESCO World Heritage site.

Eisenstadt

Visit Esterházy Palace, the former residence of the Esterházy family and a hub of musical activity during Haydn's time. Enjoy the peaceful ambiance of the town and its cultural attractions.

Carnuntum Archaeological Park

Step back in time to Roman times at this archaeological site located near Vienna. Explore ruins, reconstructed buildings, and learn about the history of the Roman settlement.

Lower Austria's Wine Regions

Lower Austria is home to several wine regions, such as the Weinviertel and Thermenregion. Embark on wine tastings, cellar tours, and immerse yourself in the local winemaking culture.

ITINERARIES

here are 10 suggested itineraries for day trips from Vienna, each offering a unique experience and a chance to explore different aspects of Austria and its neighboring countries:

Wachau Valley Delights

Morning: Depart for the Wachau Valley, a UNESCO-listed region.

Visit Melk Abbey, a magnificent Baroque structure.

Afternoon: Explore Dürnstein's charming streets and ruins.

Enjoy a leisurely lunch at a local vineyard.

Evening: Take a relaxing boat cruise on the Danube.

Imperial and Artistic Treasures

Morning: Visit Schönbrunn Palace and its gardens in Vienna.

Afternoon: Take a train to Bratislava, Slovakia.

Explore the historic Old Town, including St. Martin's Cathedral.

Evening: Return to Vienna and enjoy a cultural evening.

Musical Salzburg Experience

Morning: Take a train to Salzburg.

Visit Mozart's birthplace and the Salzburg Cathedral.

Afternoon: Explore Mirabell Palace and its gardens.

Visit Hohensalzburg Fortress for panoramic views.

Evening: Return to Vienna after a day of musical history.

Budapest Breeze

Morning: Depart by train to Budapest, Hungary.

Visit Buda Castle and Fisherman's Bastion.

Afternoon: Explore the Hungarian Parliament Building and St. Stephen's Basilica.

Enjoy traditional Hungarian cuisine for lunch.

Evening: Return to Vienna, reflecting on a day in Budapest.

Nature and Culture in Lower Austria

Morning: Head to Lower Austria's Lake Neusiedl.

Enjoy water activities or relax on the lakeside.

Afternoon: Visit Esterházy Palace in Eisenstadt.

Explore the palace and its beautiful gardens.

Evening: Return to Vienna, rejuvenated by nature and history.

Graz Adventure

Morning: Travel to Graz, Styria's capital.

Explore the charming Old Town and Hauptplatz.

Afternoon: Visit Schlossberg Hill and its clock tower.

Enjoy a traditional Styrian meal for lunch.

Evening: Return to Vienna, reminiscing about Graz's charm.

Historical Carnuntum and Roman Remains

Morning: Head to Carnuntum Archaeological Park.

Discover Roman ruins and reconstructed buildings.

Afternoon: Visit the Roman city's amphitheater and museum.

Enjoy an educational and immersive experience.

Evening: Return to Vienna, transported back in time.

Wine Regions Discovery

Morning: Choose a wine region like the Weinviertel.

Take guided tours of local wineries and vineyards.

Enjoy wine tastings and learn about winemaking.

Afternoon: Savor a vineyard lunch with local specialties.

Evening: Return to Vienna, with a new appreciation for wine.

Thermenregion Wellness and Culture

Morning: Travel to the Thermenregion wine area.

Enjoy a visit to a renowned thermal spa.

Afternoon: Visit Mayerling Hunting Lodge or Baden's casino.

Explore charming spa towns and historic sites.

Evening: Return to Vienna, relaxed and rejuvenated.

Danube Magic in Krems and Klosterneuburg

Morning: Journey to Krems, a town on the Danube.

Visit art galleries and explore the Old Town.

Afternoon: Head to Klosterneuburg.

Visit Klosterneuburg Monastery and its impressive architecture.

Evening: Return to Vienna, captivated by Danube culture.

MAPS

Vienna City Map

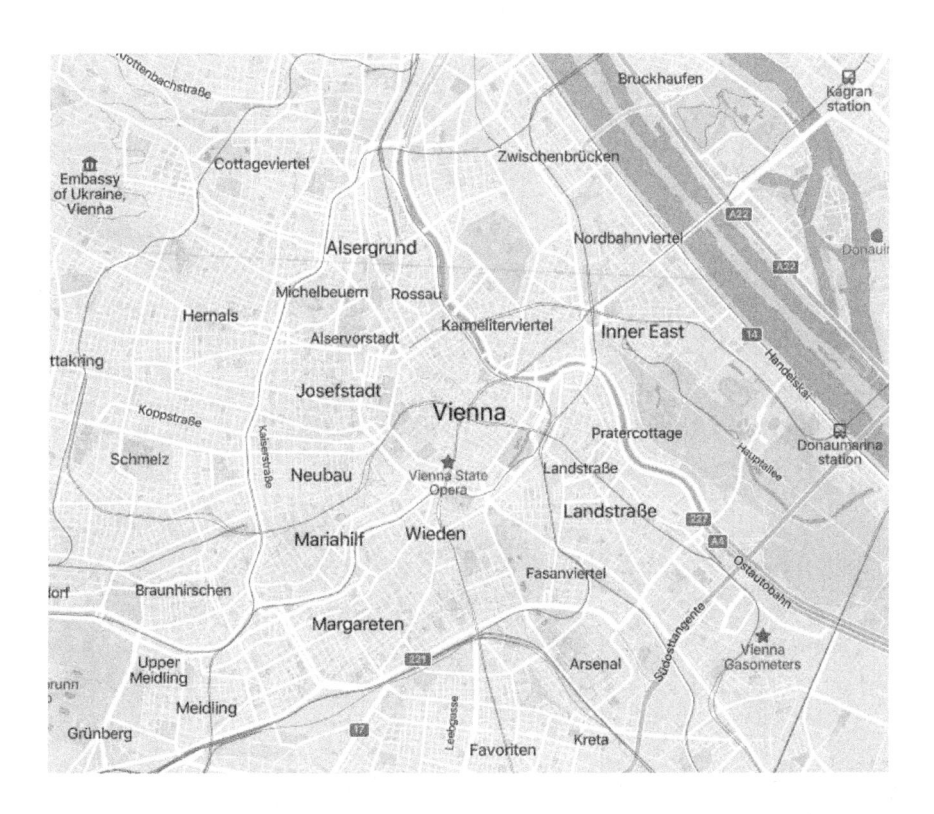

Wachau Valley Map

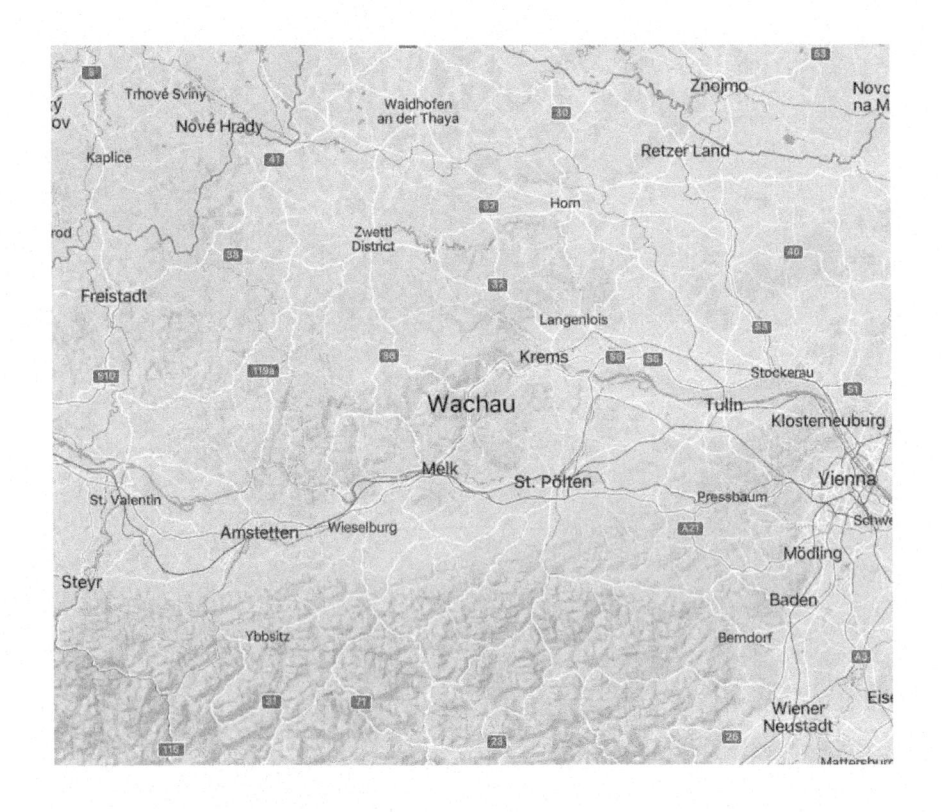

Accommodations Map

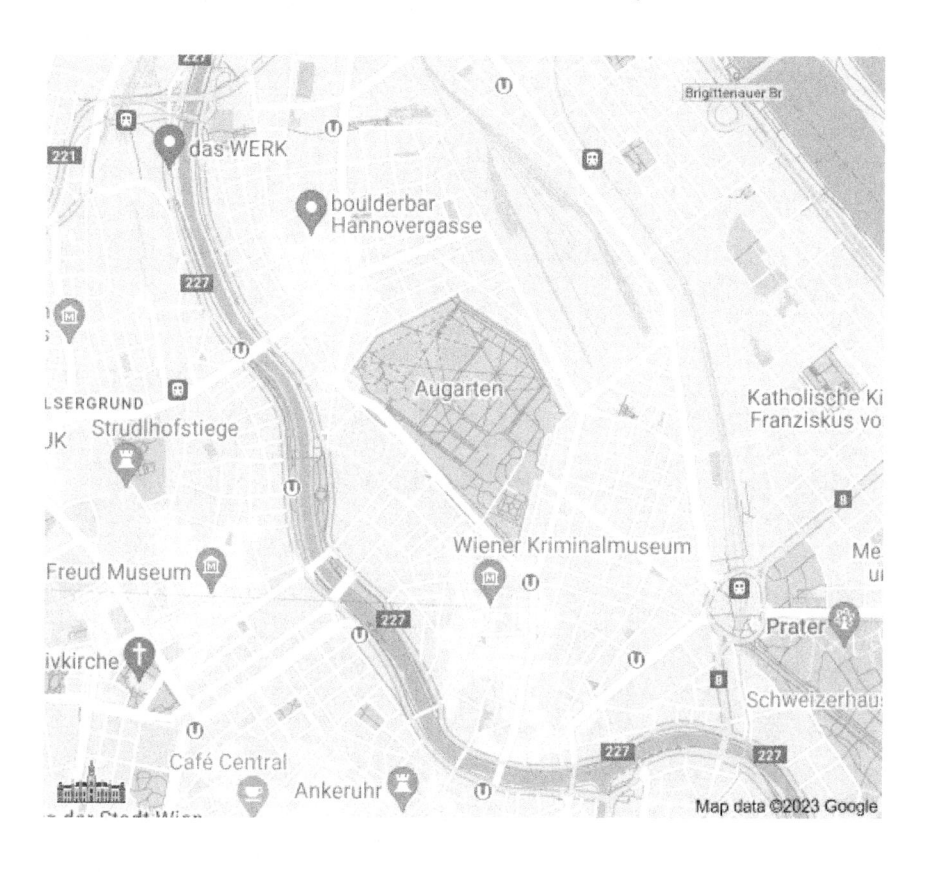

Restaurants Map

Shopping Map

CONCLUSION

As our journey through Vienna's imperial opulence comes to a close, we hope this travel guide has kindled your passion for exploration and deepened your appreciation for the cultural treasures that define this Austrian gem. Vienna is not just a destination; it's a symphony of history, a gallery of artistic masterpieces, and a stage where the past harmonizes with the present.

Whether you've marveled at the masterful strokes of Klimt's "The Kiss," experienced the grandeur of the Hofburg Palace, or simply embraced the elegance of Vienna's café culture, remember that each moment has woven itself into the fabric of your journey. As you bid farewell to this majestic city, carry with you the memories of its timeless palaces, the echoes of its musical melodies, and the spirit of a place that invites you to dream big and live grandly.

May Vienna's imperial splendor and artistic legacy continue to inspire your travels and your imagination. The memories you've gathered here will remain a source of inspiration, guiding you back whenever you seek the refinement of historical elegance, the notes of classical compositions, and the embrace of a city that elevates the senses and the soul.

INDEX

25 Travel Tips   13

A 3-Hour Journey through Schönbrunn Palace 43

A Celebration of Pastries and Delights   40

Accommodation options   11

Accommodations Map   156

Age of Enlightenment   17

Albertina   27

Albertina Museum and Art Gallery   63

An Evening of Elegance   35

Ancient and Roman Times 16

Apothecary Museum of the Vienna General Hospital   56

Austrian National Library 21

Austrian Parliament Building (Parlament)   83

Basic Information   9

Belvedere Palace (Schloss Belvedere)   50

Belvedere Palace and Museum   61

Biking 132

Bratislava, Slovakia 148

Budapest Breeze 151

Budapest, Hungary 149

Capuchin Crypt 25

Carnuntum Archaeological Park 149

Coffee Specialties 124

Cold War and Austrian Neutrality 17

Congress of Vienna and Austro-Hungarian Empire 17

Cruises 130

Cultural Events 117

Danube Magic in Krems and Klosterneuburg 153

Day Trip from Vienna to the Wachau Valley 36

Eisenstadt 149

Embark on a Journey from Vienna to Hallstatt 39

Graz 149

Graz Adventure 152

Group Activities   144

Haus der Musik (House of Music) 113

Historical Carnuntum and Roman Remains   152

Hofburg Palace   48

Hop-On Hop-Off Freedom 42

Horse-Drawn Carriage Rides   133

Hundertwasserhaus 81

Imperial and Artistic Treasures   151

Imperial Crypt (Kapuzinergruft)   53

Judenplatz Holocaust Memorial   29

Kaisergruft (Imperial Burial Vault)   59

Karlskirche (St. Charles's Church) 85

Kid-Friendly Activities   143

Kunsthistorisches Museum (Museum of Art History)   67

Lake Neusiedl   149

Leopold Museum   64

Lower Austria's Wine Regions   150

Ludwig Foundation Vienna   75

Ludwig van Beethoven   116

MAK - Austrian Museum of Applied Arts/Contemporary Art   69

Maria am Gestade   23

Medieval Era 16

Modern Vienna   18

MuseumQuartier (MQ)   71

Music Heritage   107

Musical Salzburg Experience   151

Naschmarkt   122

Nature and Culture in Lower Austria   152

Ottoman Sieges   17

Outdoor Activities   138

Pedal Through History on a Bike and City Tour 38

Rathaus (Vienna City Hall) 19

Renaissance and Baroque Period   16

Restaurants Map   157

Romantic Activities 135

Salzburg   148

Schloss Hetzendorf 52

Schönbrunn Palace (Schloss Schönbrunn)   46

Schönbrunn Palace and Gardens 148

Secession Building 72

Secession Building: Art Nouveau Showcase   87

Shopping Map   158

St. Stephen's Cathedral (Stephansdom) 77

Strolls and Hikes   128

The Spanish Riding School Experience   44

The Vienna Residence Orchestra 55

Theater And Performances 109

Thermenregion Wellness and Culture   153

Traditional Coffeehouses   120

Vienna City Map   154

Vienna State Opera 111

Vienna State Opera (Wiener Staatsoper) 79

Vienna State Opera Museum 74

Vienna's Jewish Heritage 33

Vienna's Ringstrasse 30

Viennese Sachertorte 126

Visit Vienna's Wine Taverns 137

Wachau Valley 147

Wachau Valley Delights 151

Wachau Valley Map 155

Water Sports 141

Wine Regions Discovery 152

Wolfgang Amadeus Mozart 115

World Wars and Interwar Period 17

Printed in Great Britain
by Amazon